Jazz. A Quick Immersion

Joel Dinerstein

JAZZ
A Quick Immersion

Tibidabo Publishing
New York

Published by Tibidabo Publishing, Inc. New York.

Copyediting by Lori Gerson
Cover art by Raimon Guirado
For illustration copyrights, please see page 7.

First published 2020

Visit our Series on our Web:
www.quickimmersions.com

Library of Congress Control Number: 2020940631

ISBN: 978-1-949845-15-0
2 3 4 5 6 7 8 9 10

Printed in the United States of America.

Contents

List of illustrations

Jazz is Everywhere

Jazz hides in plain sight in American music and culture. The house band at Motown were all Detroit jazz musicians. The leaders of Earth, Wind & Fire were jazz musicians who created a pop-orchestral fusion of funk, jazz, soul, and disco. Ray Charles played something we might call soul jazz; Steely Dan was a jazz rock band. The seminal rock-and-roll hits of Fats Domino were recorded in New Orleans by a house band of swing-era jazz musicians; Parliament Funkadelic worked within a jazz model of collective improvisation. The house bands of the Memphis soul labels were jazz musicians, whether Booker T. Jones and the Memphis Horns (at Stax) or Al Green's rhythm section (at Hi Records). Both Charlie Watts and Ginger Baker were professional jazz drummers before creating the deep grooves of Cream and the Rolling Stones. Stevie Wonder's first album was entitled *The Jazz Soul of Little Stevie* and his hit "Sir Duke" was a tribute to Duke Ellington. Jay-Z's first nickname was "Jazzy" and the aesthetic concept of "flow" —its rhythmic mastery— is just another repercussion of the music's influence.

Jazz started as a rhythmic revolution out of New Orleans and later took on its current concert form of expressive virtuosic solos. Jazz created the groove and pocket —the rhythmic foundation— of nearly all American music. Without jazz? —no soul, no funk, no modern blues, no rock-&-roll, no hiphop, no torch singing, no Afro-futurism, no Western swing. Without jazz arranger and producer Quincy Jones, no *Thriller* or *Off the Wall*. Without Thundercat and Kamasi Washington, no *To Pimp a Butterfly*.

Jazz was America's popular music for three decades (1917-1947) and emerged as part of a pop-music continuum that included blues, ragtime, vaudeville, minstrelsy, and even carnival music. In the 1920s, jazz was the container for this roiling caldron of popular musical forms, just as today jazz combines with funk, hiphop, soul, R&B, EDM, and electronica. The small R&B combos were carved out of the swing-era's big bands then morphed into rock-and-roll; saxophone solos were the model for electric guitar solos.

Jazz is an art form of musical interplay and ensemble individuality. To put it another way, jazz is the self-expression of the solo grounded in the textures of the ensemble. A short definition: *jazz is the individual sounding of human experience expressed within a supportive group.*

Jazz is the deep structure of American music where every individual gets the chance to speak their piece in real time. When listening to any jazz performance, find the groove or follow the soloist. In short time, you will be able to do both and the composition will open up.

This book is for readers without musical knowledge and my thesis is simple: jazz is a profound art form and it will enhance your life. Bassist Charlie Haden once explained jazz this way: "We're actually fulfilling a calling to a responsibility to the universe. And that is to make beautiful music, and bring beauty and deeper values to people's lives, so that they can touch the deeper parts inside themselves".

Improvising is the artistic coin of the jazz realm and life itself is an ongoing improvisation. "Improvisation teaches you the magic of being in the moment you're living in", Haden said. "And you see yourself in relation to the universe in a completely different way. There's only right now, when you're improvising".

There are Spotify playlists to guide each chapter. Consider listening first to the one called "Jazz Beauty", performances that need little introduction. To get started, here are some elements to guide your listening.

Jazz is a Conversation

Jazz musicians are having a conversation together —a nightly, improvised, non-verbal conversation when live or a literal record of a musical dialogue. Conversation is the dominant metaphor of the art form, as musicologist Paul Berliner found in his epic ethnography, *Thinking in Jazz: The Infinite Art of Improvisation.*

Jazz musicians have often been said to "talk" on their instruments, especially the horn players. The reference point for jazz musicians is not the notes written on the page (as with classical musicians) nor any sense of "correct" playing (as in traditional folk music). Rather, the model of the jazz solo is the human voice itself. Jazz is musical conversation and the soloing musician has the floor. During a solo, the other voices support, challenge, and offer new paths.

In the early 1900s, African-American jazz musicians *vocalized* their instruments by accompanying blues singers or transmuting the tone and phrasing of gospel singers. In early jazz, musicians used mutes or derbies to vary an instrument's pitch or volume, calibrating it to the human voice's micro-tones. To be able to cry, moan, slur, shout, and growl on one's instrument became part of the jazz toolkit. In addition, many had played in circus, carnival, or minstrel bands: making improper sounds for humor on horns was part of those traditions. Vocalizing instruments remains central to jazz through joyful cries, ecstatic moans, or even the imitation of bodily sounds.

To hear this, check out how trombonist "Tricky" Sam Nanton makes his horn sound like a human voice in the opening measures of Duke Ellington's "Chloe" or thirty seconds into "Ko-Ko". Listen to the opening horn riff of Count Basie's "Blues in the Dark": incredibly these are instruments, not human voices. To hear how a tenor saxophone testifies, as if in church, listen to Greg Hardy's solo on Bill Frisell's version of "A Change is Gonna Come" (@ 4:00).

With the human voice as their North Star, jazz musicians increased the range, technique and tonal palette of nearly every instrument. Louis Armstrong created the modern sound of the trumpet and Coleman Hawkins, the tenor saxophone. Thelonious Monk heard the piano as a drum and sounded out its percussive potential. Jazz musicians have always adapted their instruments to their own individual artistic visions.

Jazz is the Art of Improvisation

Improvisation is the act of *spontaneous composition* within a song's structure. It can be done as a solo performance or in conversation with others or by singers. For New Orleans drummer Johnny Vidacovitch, improvisation is "one hundred *nano-split-second* forks in the road". Each one will take the song or performance in a different direction and the drummer, in particular, has to decide if or how to direct the soloist or the groove. Improvisation is the main artistic challenge of jazz as an art form.

Pianist Keith Jarrett often sits down at a concert piano with nothing but a few thematic ideas and performs hour-long improvisational solo concerts. On his most popular and iconic live recording —*The Koln Concert*— Jarrett caps an hourlong set with a stunning resolution: Part IV is a complete composition with a beautiful melody, steady underlying rhythm, imaginative variations, heartbreaking climax, slow recovery, and triumphant finish.

Pianist Bill Evans once described improvisation in jazz as analogous to a genre of Japanese black-ink painting. In this technique (*sumi-e*), an artist puts his or her brush to paper and does not pick it back up until the work is finished: neither revisions nor edits are allowed. This puts the emphasis on creating intuitive structures for one's improvisational explorations. Consider jazz a set of five or six such artists in a room, where each one's drawing affects the others, micro-second by micro-second.

In fact, this is exactly how the Miles Davis Quintet created *Kind of Blue,* the best-selling jazz album of all time. There were no rehearsals and just two quick run-throughs: musicians saw the compositions for the first time in the studio. Davis called the tune and everyone played until each song ended. No second takes, no overdubs, no studio fixes. He wanted the spontaneity of these virtuosos —the newness, the nervousness, the first contact with these ideas— to carry the piece from start to finish.

Music critic Whitney Balliett called jazz "the sound of surprise" —whether its initial rhythmic surprise of syncopation, those in-the-moment thrills of a solo, or the wondrous tensions of the groove's conversation. When Louis Armstrong ripped upward to a higher note —*surprise!*— he defied every proper idea of pure tone, lyricism, or correct playing. When Miles Davis brought funk, rock, and electronic instruments into jazz —*surprise!*— many fans and musicians wondered whether it was even jazz. When the sci-fi choir soars in on Kamasi Washington's "Change of the Guard", a listener may wonder, "where the hell did they come from?" Expect surprise.

For some listeners, it may be easier to understand improvisation through the genre's vocalists: Billie Holiday, Frank Sinatra, Tony Bennett, Ella Fitzgerald, Nina Simone, Anita O'Day, Chet Baker, Dinah Washington, Nat King Cole, Sarah Vaughan. Their jazz heirs include Cassandra Wilson, Diana Krall, Gregory Porter, Joni Mitchell, Dianne Reeves, Cécile McLorin Salvant, Harry Connick, Jr., Kurt Elling, and Melody Gardot. How do singers improvise and create "the sound of surprise?"

The jazz vocalist's art concerns rhythm above all —how to swing a song, how to match syllable to note, how to move in-and-out of the groove. "Keeping in time, in jazz, is even more important than keeping in tune", Will Friedwald wrote in *Jazz*

Singing. To drop *behind* the beat sets the singer out-of-sync with the band: this creates drama, as if the singer is living the lyrics of the song and the band is listening. (This is a strategy of Sinatra and Billie Holiday). Or the vocalist might rush the beat such that the band hurries to keep up, creating humor and anticipation. (This is a strategy of Louis Armstrong and Dinah Washington).

The impact of jazz vocalists is deeply embedded in all pop singing. That is why so many pop, rock, and country singers challenge themselves to record an album of jazz standards, whether Willie Nelson or Linda Ronstadt, Seal or Rod Stewart, Gloria Estefan or Bob Dylan.

Jazz, Freedom, and Voice

A jazz musician must create a signature sound —a personalized voice— on his or her instrument. This is the very definition of a jazz musician, the art form's aesthetic imperative. As Louis Armstrong declared in 1932, "I determined from the start to cultivate an original style and I tried out all sorts of ideas, discarding some, practicing others, until I reached, not perfection … but the best that was in me". Jazz musicians found a non-verbal pathway to freedom, a term often invoked in jazz innovation.

Jazz and Freedom

Jazz represents the birth of an art form from the maelstrom of oppression —this, too, is one of its key stories. African-American jazz musicians repudiated the colonized past to lead a reclamation project of culture and heritage. Toni Morrison always claimed to be "chasing the musicians", and her novel, *Jazz,* is a tribute. "Musicians have fired my imagination as much as anything in literature", author Ernest Gaines once said, such as "the understatement of Lester Young and the crying, haunting, forever searching sounds of John Coltrane".

Here are two key years (1960-61) of this freedom story during the early civil rights movement. In 1960, drummer Max Roach and jazz vocalist Abbey Lincoln released *We Insist!,* the first album in any musical genre to confront slavery. Songs like "Driva Man" and "Freedom Day" recalled the traumatic experience and emancipation; then "In Africa", Lincoln chanted the ancestral tribal names of cultural heritage —Bantu, Congo, Dahomey, Yoruba, Zulu. A year later, the John Coltrane Quartet recorded *Africa/Brass*, an album of musical bridges across the middle passage: "Africa" is a 16-minute immersion with polyrhythms, vocalized whoops, and deep brass blends; "Greensleeves", the traditional English folk song, is Africanized through saxophone and drums; "Blues Minor" represents the bedrock form of African-American experience; "Song of the Underground Railroad" is a propulsive remembrance of those who escaped. Then a year later came Oliver Nelson's *Blues and the Abstract Truth*: he allowed his musicians "maximum freedom" in their solos while the title declares the philosophical depth of African-American musical forms.

Jazz began as an African-American artistic form but its practices have constantly been adapted and reshaped by musicians all over the world. "I've always felt that the music started out as black", (white) guitarist Jim Hall reflected, "but that it's as much mine now as anyone else's. I haven't stolen the music from anybody —I just bring something different to it". Trumpeter Rex Stewart once said of (white) baritone saxophonist Gerry Mulligan: "He has soul, and he plays and talks like a man who enjoys life and people. I felt a kinship with him right away. If a man doesn't feel him, he must be dead". Any authentic musician is one immersed in a tradition, who has mastered its canon and values, and who acts as a representative of the art form.

Jazz is the record of one person's individual struggle and experience etched in sound.

Cities, Sonics, and Jazz Beauty

This book is organized in two unequal sections: cities and sonics.

Joel Dinerstein

QIJ - Introduction

Created by Joel Dinerstein · 12 songs, 1 hr 9 min

PLAY

FOLLOWERS 9

Download

#	TITLE	ARTIST	ALBUM		
	I'm Gonna Move to the Outskirts of Town	Ray Charles, Andy Ra...	Jazz for Dance Floors	2020-04-22	3:46
	East St. Louis Toodle-Oo	Steely Dan	Pretzel Logic	2020-04-22	2:47
	Sir Duke	Stevie Wonder	Songs In The Key Of L...	2020-04-22	3:53
	Complexion (A Zulu Love)	Kendrick Lamar, Raps...	To Pimp A Butterfly	2020-04-22	4:23
	Chloe (Song of the Swamp) - 1999 Remastered	Duke Ellington	Never No Lament: Th...	2020-04-22	3:25
	A Change Is Gonna Come	Bill Frisell	History, Mystery	2019-03-19	8:49
	Freddie Freeloader	Miles Davis	Kind Of Blue	2020-04-22	9:46
	Last Train To Clarksville	Cassandra Wilson	New Moon Daughter	2020-04-22	5:17
	Freedom Day	Abbey Lincoln	Remember 1959-1961...	2020-04-22	6:03
	Greensleeves	John Coltrane Quartet	The Complete Africa...	2019-06-02	10:01
	Stolen Moments	Oliver Nelson	The Blues and the Abs...	2019-04-09	8:45
	Wrap Your Troubles In Dreams (And Dream Y...	Frank Sinatra	Swing Easy!	2019-06-02	2:13

1. Dinerstein's Introduction playlist.

The five main chapters explore the main developments of jazz in specific American cities. Each chapter is a field guide to the jazz developments there through five or six short sections. There is a playlist for each city and analyses for the innovative jazz elements of each historical era.

Jazz absorbed the spirit and sounds of every region in America: born and developed in New Orleans, sharpened and organized in Chicago, jammed and swung hard in Kansas City, busted wide open by bebop innovators in New York City, chilled and later funkified in Los Angeles. Musicians in Europe, Africa, and Asia integrated the innovations and always brought something new to the musical table.

The second, *sonic* half is comprised of playlists that illuminate how the art form works. Each focuses on a key element of jazz performance: *the groove; the ensemble; the blues; sound and solo; jazz beauty.* My intention here is to create and instill musical maps in the mind of readers and listeners.

Jazz abounds in artistic beauty: trio interplay, orchestral colors, rhythmic complexity, fiery trumpets, the human cry of the saxophone, the brass blasting power of big bands. Jazz beauty is the signature sound of Miles Davis' muted trumpet, the springy bass of Esperanza Spalding, Billie Holiday's one-act vocal dramas, Sonny Rollins' saxophone spirals. There is also the rougher beauty of Ornette Coleman's alto wailings, Sun Ra's Afro-futurist jamming, Herbie Hancock's liquid electronics, Carla

Bley's complex arrangements. There is the lyricism of pianists in dialogue with horns: McCoy Tyner and John Coltrane, John Hicks and David Murray, Alice Coltrane and Pharoah Sanders.

Jazz was the first global popular music before World War II and then musicians transformed it into the first *global* music. Dizzy Gillespie created Latin jazz through Afro-Cuban musicians and drummers. John Coltrane brought African and Indian rhythms into jazz. Stan Getz helped create bossa nova jazz, presaging the influence of Brazilian music in the 1970s. Norway's ECM label brought Scandinavian approaches to space, silence, and acoustics into jazz. Chinese, Japanese, and Indian musicians are in the first rank of jazz's current generation.

Jazz is American, ethnic, national, hemispheric, global, diasporic.

A final listening note: no matter the density or intensity of any jazz composition, listen for how the soloist surfs through the musical storm. A jazz musician creates a voice and perspective, speaks his or her piece, finds harmony with others, fights the overwhelming social and economic forces, achieves moments of beauty and clarity, then bows out to allow the next person to speak. This struggle is symbolic of any individual's everyday battle and it is also, roughly translated, one way to understand the call-and-response between the soloist and supporting ensemble.

Jazz is a story of art, aesthetics, race, freedom, ethnic culture, and individual expression.

Many people think jazz is difficult to understand —that it is abrasive, cerebral chamber music or hard to follow— but *jazz is everywhere*. A listener need only become aware of a few elements to understand any jazz performance. So now we point our ears first towards New Orleans, the most cosmopolitan musical city in America at the turn of the twentieth century.

Chapter 1

New Orleans: A Public Music of the Streets

At small adjacent parks on the edge of New Orleans two bands often battled in 1906, Buddy Bolden's and Papa John Robichaux's. At Lincoln Park, Robichaux's seven-piece society band played sweet melodies with jaunty rhythms, a pastoral sound of picnics and jitneys, spiked with the occasional embellished phrase on violin or clarinet. At Johnson Park, Bolden watched from a small bandstand elevated over the baseball fields, waiting for a crowd to gather. He would whisper to his trombonist, "OK, now let's call our children home", and they would shout their signature riff, syncopating its rhythm —"ragging it", as it was called— playing it over and over until it hit

Robichaux's crowd. People would then drift over, as if the instruments were brass magnets.

People recall that Bolden's sound sometimes floated three miles down from Carrollton to the French Quarter and Treme. This is more geography than hyperbole: New Orleans is almost flat and musicians say its humid, heavy air carries music farther than in most cities. People would catch the song on the wind, recognize the sound —"Hey, Buddy Bolden's playing"— then get on the streetcar or hitch a ride.

Robichaux's band beat Bolden a few times in musical battle but only when he brought in a ringer —Manuel Perez, a Creole trumpeter and leader of the popular Onward Brass Band. The Onward featured the distinctive, "hot" two-trumpet attack of Perez and Joe "King" Oliver, Louis Armstrong's mentor. "Hot music" was a synonym for jazz until 1945, a term lost to public memory yet key to understanding the excitement triggered by jazz.

The sound of modernity was coming in on the wind from Lincoln Park, Black men blowing loud, rough, strong, syncopated instrumental blues, improvising without a score.

The Soundscape of Modernity

What do you hear in New Orleans jazz that sounds like modernity? First, *bang!* —a collective rhythmic upthrust— and three horns jump in playing separate lines. They swirl around each other at first and it can be disorienting: it is best to follow the trumpet's lead with your ears and the banjo's beat with your feet. Once oriented to the swirling musical lines, listen for the clarinet as it soars into the higher register and the wry, mocking phrases on the trombone. After the first chaotic section, there will be two or three solos while the tuba and banjo maintain a steady beat; a transition to a new section is often marked by a circus or carnival riff. After the solos, there is a joyous out-chorus at the end: all the instruments rejoin and chase each other hell-for-leather, like runners for the finish line. (*King Oliver's "Dippermouth Blues" is a good example*).

So why did jazz start in New Orleans at the turn of the twentieth century?

Jazz was a grass-roots music that developed in New Orleans when Southern Blacks had neither political voice nor access to the ballot. When the first jazz recordings swept the nation in 1917, white supremacy was the law in Louisiana, lynching was at its peak, and the South was strictly segregated. The white elites of New Orleans actually disowned jazz due to its Black origins, rhythmic emphasis, and lack of refinement. The vibrant, exciting music offended the Southern city's genteel Victorian artistic ethos of sweetness and light. The *New Orleans Times-Picayune* called it nothing more than "the beat of the tom-tom drums", a novelty music for the lower classes, "a kind of servants' hall of rhythm". In an editorial, the newspaper warned its readers that jazz was a plague: "its musical value is nil, and its possibilities of harm are great".

In contrast, New Orleans musicians considered jazz an artistic form of freedom. In clarinetist Sidney Bechet's essential memoir, *Treat It Gentle,* he called the feeling of improvising alongside other musicians "freedom", whether soloing or in solidarity: "*all that freedom,* all that feeling a man's got when he's playing next to you.. [there's] all that closeness of speaking to another instrument, to another man". Equality on the bandstand offered the first generation of African-American jazz musicians their only chance to speak in public with "all that pride and spirit". As composer Duke Ellington would say later, "Jazz had to say what we [Blacks] couldn't say".

New Orleans jazz is inseparable from the city's living traditions of public music, of parading, of drumming and dancing in the streets. "That's the heartbeat of New Orleans, the parade, I love a parade", early jazz banjoist and guitarist Danny Barker once said, "because this is a good-time town, it's a 24-hour town. Don't have no curfew here. You know, in the *Treme* [neighborhood], they ready right now to strike up a band". Barker here refers to the weekly festive rituals of community and identity known as second lines that have marked turf and neighborhood in African-American communities since just after the Civil War. As apprentices, Louis Armstrong carried King Oliver's trumpet on parades, Bechet followed his teachers, and Barker followed his grandfather Isidore Barbarin in the Onward Brass Band. All three later played in second lines.

This horn-powered brass-band music of the streets can still be heard every Sunday on second lines, now funked up by the Rebirth Brass Band or the Hot 8, TBC or the Soul Rebels. Sunday second line parades are four-hour, four-mile rolling block parties through African-American neighborhoods powered by brass bands and followed by crowds of three hundred or more. These parades harken back to West African rituals and variations also exist in the Afro-Caribbean.

New Orleans jazz is and was a social music of the streets, a collective sounding built upon the traditional African dialogue of dancers and drummers. "What made that music possible was the people", Bechet recalled. "The people knew what they wanted to hear and *the musicianers* gave it to them… If the music was being played right, the people would know it". It was a *public sounding*: bands drove through the city playing on flatbed trucks, stopping to challenge other bands on corners. Swing-era saxophonist Lester Young recalled from his youth: "In New Orleans they had them trucks that go round [with bands] and advertise for a dance …. and this excited me, you know? So I'd be the handbill boy running around and I just loved that music… Every time they'd start to play, anything I was doing, they start playing some music —Boom! I'd run there".

The objective of New Orleans jazz musicians was to encourage a unifying spirit in every environment, whether on the streets, in clubs, or on stages. Their most rewarding moments came when audiences of everyday people responded with emotion, enthusiasm, and physical grace in dance. As listeners, we can hear this spirit of the streets —and Bechet's feeling of freedom— in the music's flexible rhythmic grooves. Once aligned with the rhythm, a listener hears with more clarity the joyful collaboration of the musicians, the clarinet soaring over the ensemble, the banjo strumming underneath.

This call-and-response of the streets exists in jazz as an integral musical element: a musician sends out a solo call and a group of instruments responds with encouragement. There is an accessible example in Bessie Smith's iconic version of "St. Louis Blues" (1925): her grief acts as a call for Louis Armstrong's instrumental response as it reflects her emotion. She sings, "I hate to see / that evenin' su-u-u-n go down" and the trumpet offers a sympathetic phrase, as if saying "tell me about it". Smith repeats the line with a darker inflection the second time ("I hate to *see-ee-ee*") and Armstrong's quick, light phrase says simply, "I'm listening". By the second verse, as the singer considers leaving town, "If I'm feelin' tomorrow / like I feel today", Armstrong deepens his emotional response by moaning back to her. We are now in the midst of a conversation, a duet, a *blues-call* and *jazz-response*.

With jazz, as with blues, African-Americans found musical ways to protest their oppression in coded form. Yet the music was innovative, original, and well-adapted to "the tempo of modern life", a resonant phrase of the 1920s. As Quincy Jones always said, "Music has to reflect the tempo of the times".

New Orleans' "Extreme Multiculturalism"

Jazz begins in New Orleans because drums were banned to slaves in every Southern state but Louisiana. Slave-owners knew people of African descent could send messages through rhythmic patterns. The South Carolina law read, "It is absolutely necessary to the safety of this Province, that all due care be taken to restrain Negroes from using or keeping of drums"; Georgia banned all "drums, horns, or other loud instruments, which may give sign or notice of wicked designs or intentions". This urban music of the streets could only have started in a city where drums were legal and where African drummers and dancers imported Havana's habanera beat (a key source of syncopation). All this happened in Congo Square, America's most important historical music site.

Congo Square was the main portal of African drumming and dancing traditions as transmitted into US culture. On Sundays in the early nineteenth century, slaves were given the day off and created a marketplace where they played the traditional rhythms and dances of their specific African ethnic groups —Congo, Yoruba, Senegambia— to affirm their cultural heritage. At Congo Square, slaves made extra money selling food and clothing while walking around *stylin'* innovative African-*American* gestures, attitudes, and dances. New rhythmic cross-pollinations were created, a *pan*-African set of innovations: men played congas, slit-drums, and djembes; male and female dancers wearing bells and ankle bracelets transmitted the percussive African past into their American present.

Congo Square was a tourist attraction throughout the nineteenth century and a new musical hybrid emerged there of African, Caribbean, and European music and dances. New Orleans jazz is less an "African" music than an "Afro-US form" (Albert Murray's phrase), created from an unrecoverable set of cultural exchanges. Now a section of Armstrong Park, Congo Square is one birthplace of American popular music.

New Orleans was also the most cosmopolitan American city of the nineteenth century with a majority Black population, an example of "extreme multiculturalism, extraordinarily early" in historian Richard Campanella's words. The city was colonized by France, governed by Spain (1762-1803), and bought by the US in 1803. New Orleans was the second largest US port between 1830-1870, the largest city in the US South, and a major domestic slave market. New Orleans music developed through trade and cultural circulation within the Caribbean; Havana and New Orleans were "sister cities". The city's main African populations were Senegambian and Kongo-Angola, both powerful African culture complexes. The city's educated, mixed-race Creole caste was reinforced by French refugees from the Haitian Revolution in the early 1800s. There was a major wave of Irish immigration before the Civil War and a major wave of Italian immigration a generation after the war, along with smaller groups of Germans, Greeks, and Jews; many early jazz musicians were Irish, Italian, and Jewish. The city's musical culture was rivaled only by New York's: it had two opera houses, two orchestras, and several theaters along with a public culture of dancing and vendors' cries on the streets.

Jazz was a creolized music cooked up out of ragtime piano, Afro-Cuban rhythms, John Philip Sousa's brass band music, Italian operatic arias, military drum patterns, Creole songs, Afro-Caribbean rhythms, and French courtly dances, as it all converged with the popular music of vaudeville and circus bands. Tango and Hispanic rhythms deserve special emphasis: "if you can't manage to put tinges of Spanish in your tunes", Jelly Roll

Morton said, "you will never be able to get the right seasoning, I call it, for jazz". Jazz was also a cross-class music among African-Americans, a musical exchange between former slaves and mixed-race Creoles, improvisers and so-called "reading musicians". This combination of musical elements, heritage, and social factors existed only in New Orleans.

Here were musicians used to parading in the streets, providing rhythmic uplift in any environment, and in dialogue with much of the world's music. New Orleans produced jazz's first major composer (Jelly Roll Morton), its first master soloists (Louis Armstrong, Sidney Bechet, trombonist Kid Ory), and its first small jazz groups built on a brass-band foundation.

The city's instrumental traditions are ongoing: there is a trumpet tradition, from Armstrong to Wynton Marsalis to Nicholas Payton; a piano line, from Jelly Roll Morton to Professor Longhair to Allen Toussaint; a drum tradition, from Baby Dodds to Ed Blackwell to Herlin Riley of the Lincoln Center Jazz Orchestra. This genealogy extends back into the pre-recorded past: Buddy Bolden's powerful cornet "calling his children home", legendary pianist Tony Jackson playing in Storyville bordellos, and Armstrong's favorite street bass drummer, Black Benny, rolling people along second lines with his strong left hand.

The 1920s: The Jazz Age Meets The Machine Age

Writers often pointed to the new triad of *jazz, cities, and machines* in the 1920s. Jazz was propulsive, rhythmic, noisy dance music from 1917-1945, a fact since obscured by its current nightclub form. The classical composer Daniel Mason attacked jazz as "ultra-modernistic" due to its "relentless mechanical efficiency" and compared it to how "robots would make a music of their own". He was trying to hold onto the violin-centered sentimental music of social elites when the new industrial soundscape called for a more vital aesthetic to reflect mechanical repetition, power, volume, and perpetual motion. Here is the key convergence: The 1920s were called "The Jazz Age" for the music's rapid, spirited tempo while art historians call it "the Machine Age", referring to a new aesthetic of precision, noise, and repetition. In effect, jazz was the popular music of the Machine Age, as I showed in my cultural history of early jazz, *Swinging the Machine.*

Jazz was the popular music of 1920s college youth while it helped immigrants and urbanites adapt to the urban, industrial soundscape. Jewish immigrant songwriter Irving Berlin wrote in 1924 that jazz was "the rhythmic beat of our everyday lives", and that its "swiftness is interpretive of our [American] verve and speed and ceaseless activity". Classical pianist Leop-

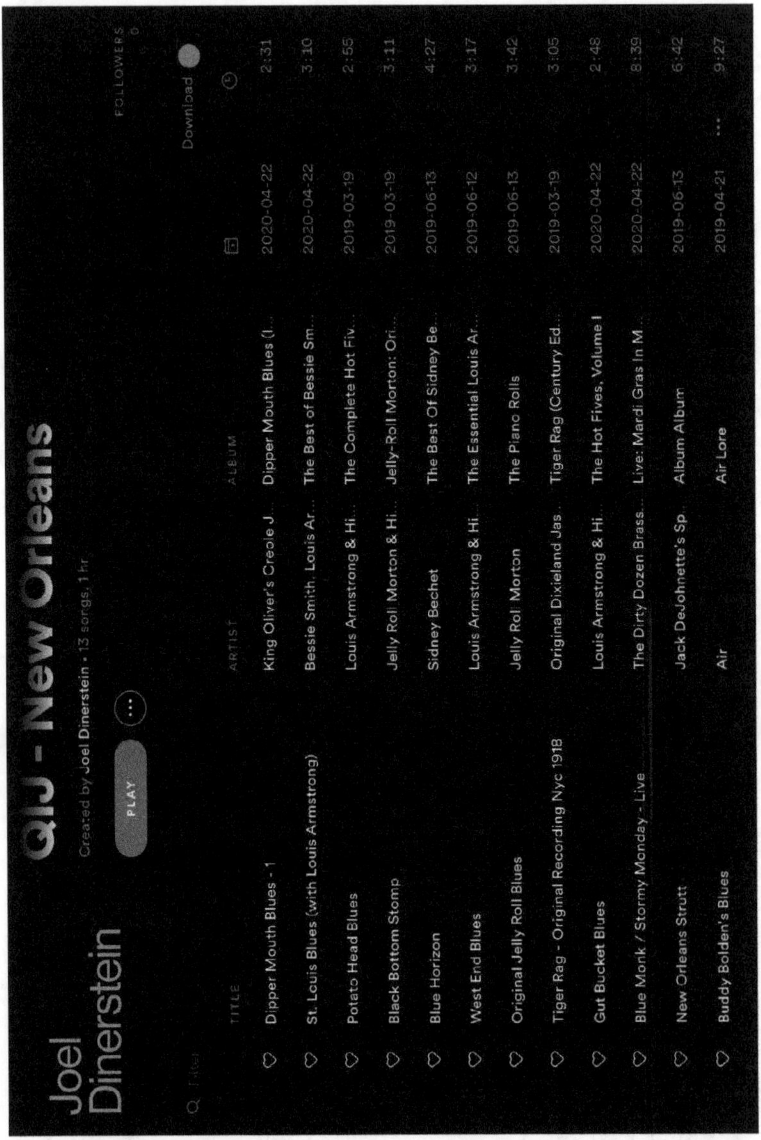

2. Dinerstein's New Orleans playlist.

old Godowsky noted that, in terms of sonic power, "one tenor saxophone is equal to eight violas" and the drummer worked "a dozen noisy devices" —such reflections of jazz's sonic power were common. Bandleader Paul Whiteman said he heard steamboats, locomotives and electricity in jazz— he meant it positively; critic H.L. Mencken said he heard "the sound of riveting" in jazz rhythms —he meant it negatively.

New Orleans jazz was an uptempo, disruptive music of steady and syncopated rhythms, a musical form able to reflect modernity's noise, chaos, and mechanical repetition into an original kind of dance music allowing for individual voices and group drive. The appeal of New Orleans music was in talking back to the industrial rhythms of trains and trolleys, movies and radio, cars and trucks. Forty years of European immigration and rural-to-urban migration had created a younger generation hungry for a new American musical tempo geared to modern city life.

Listening to New Orleans Jazz

Here are the key elements of New Orleans jazz: *polyphony, syncopated rhythm, stop-time, the break, the out-chorus, call-and-response.* Polyphony literally means "many lines": the front-line horns play separate melodies and improvise collectively. *Syncopation* means off-beat rhythmic emphasis —that is, where you don't expect it. *Stop-time* is literal: the flow stops and all instruments play in unison on the beat to support a soloist. *The break* is a climactic moment: all the musicians fall out and the main soloist carries the song into the next section. The *out-chorus* is a final burst of collective improvisation and impressive group enthusiasm.

The two case studies here are "Potato Head Blues" by Louis Armstrong's Hot Seven and "Black Bottom Stomp" by Jelly Roll Morton and his Red Hot Peppers. Each has a combination of the elements listed above. And listen for onomatopoetic, humorous sounds —whether of cars or horses— since jazz was in active dialogue with the soundscape.

In "Potato Head Blues", Armstrong plays a relaxed melody line aligned with the tuba's slow parade beat while the clarinet soars above as if chasing the trumpet. This is a *duel* rather than a *duet*, its melodic tension mediated by the banjo's time-keeping. At 1:04, the clarinet takes a solo, mostly in the upper register, adding a few humorous slurs and slides. The banjo then strums alone for twelve beats, setting up Armstrong for a famously masterful solo (at 1:50). He improvises a new melody line, mixing lyrical phrasing with bent and held long notes; he creates drama with an explosive riff then backs off to relax in his own rhythmic ease. Towards the end of the solo, Armstrong rips up to a spiked high note then descends into the arms of the waiting ensemble as if coming home. The rousing out-chorus (at 2:32) sounds like the band's celebration of its own achievement.

Armstrong's solo embodies artistic individuality, freedom, dignity, and control —all of which were unavailable in his daily life. In contrast, two years later, Armstrong had a hit singing "(What Did I Do To Be So) Black and Blue?" This is a song that equates being black with being beaten and bruised —*black and blue*— and Armstrong's vocal has a pathos absent from his instrumental mastery. "I'm white / *inside*/ but that don't help my case", he sings "because I / *ca-an't* help / what is in my face". Armstrong was able to assert his artistic power in jazz and *feel* the freedom denied him in a white supremacist society: "my only sin", he sings, "is in my skin".

The second example is Jelly Roll Morton's "Black Bottom Stomp". This composition has a surprise every ten seconds: dynamic breaks, propulsive transitions, odd juxtapositions, stop-time, slap-bass, call-and-response, explosive riffs. The *riff* is central to jazz: it is a short, repeated rhythmic phrase often introduced early to work as the "glue" of the composition.

"Black Bottom Stomp" races out of the gate with a circus riff played by the ensemble *twice* in eight seconds! The tempo is moderated slightly by a relaxed counter-riff paced by the string-bass. The trumpet emerges with a short, crisp solo and the ensemble answers in a fine example of *call-and-response,* their phrases overlapping. A piercing clarinet riff echoes the trumpet's and the whole ensemble rejoins for a short slapstick phrase. A wry trombone riff leads the ensemble into a rollicking rhythm for twenty seconds (@ 1:00): trumpet and clarinet alternate while the trombone mouths off like the peanut gallery. A short, jaunty clarinet solo picks up the pace and then suddenly all the instruments drop out: Jelly Roll Morton's barroom piano solo (@1:33) owns the break with an embellished ragtime figure. The trumpet follows with a stop-time solo, adding syncopation and a bit of the Charleston (2:02). A jangling, strumming banjo then takes over, spurred on by the drums and slap-bass. The clarinet then calls the trumpet and trombone back (2:34) until the rhythm section rejoins for a joyous *out-chorus* (2:49) —then it's a race to the finish until we're all pounding the table.

These men were virtuosos of this new modernist music. For an improvisational concerto, listen to Bechet's "Blue Horizon", a four-minute moody blues that alternates between deep moaning and ecstatic cries. For how a short, thrilling solo raised the bar of jazz improvisation, listen to Armstrong's groundbreaking 12-second intro to "West End Blues". For an ear-opening journey from ragtime to jazz via blues, listen to Jelly Roll Morton's "Original Jelly Roll Blues" (1924), so modern it still sounds like New Orleans today. In Woody Allen's *Manhattan,* the main character names "Potato Head Blues" as one reason to stay alive: as with all art, the vitality and artistry of Armstrong, Bechet, and Morton uplifted minds, bodies, and spirits.

Kings of Jazz, Real and Commercial

Ironically, it was a white band that brought about the jazz revolution in 1917 during a six-week residency at New York's Reisenweber's Restaurant: the Original Dixieland Jass Band. Their songs were characterized by a frenetic pace, polyphony that seemed out of control, and novelty sounds wrested from their instruments. The ODJB's "Livery Stable Blues" was one of the first million-selling records and "Tiger Rag" was equally popular. The ODJB was led by cornetist Nick LaRocca and clarinetist Larry Shields, the sons of Italian and Irish immigrants, respectively. The band's hit records transformed popular music, social dance, and night-club culture. New York bandleader Vincent Lopez declared that "the advent of Dixieland on Broadway changed the fabric of the entertainment world", away from "schmaltzy music with heart appeal" to jazz, "[which] does something to the adrenal glands!" The rhythmic drive of New Orleans jazz transformed the nation's musical culture in a complex story of music, dance, race, marketing, and industrialization.

The first so-called "King of Jazz" was Paul Whiteman, a man proclaimed "Entertainer of the Year" by *Variety* magazine for 1921-1922. A former symphony violinist, Whiteman created a national franchise of well-rehearsed commercial big bands and became the public face of jazz. Famous for his "businessman's bounce", Whiteman turned jazz's small-band vitality into dance music for bourgeois hotel nightlife. He gave a famous concert at New York's Town Hall in 1924 with the stated intention of "making a lady out of jazz" —this was a coded phrase suggesting the necessity of refining the raw music of Black New Orleanians by muting its rhythmic power. This concert also catapulted composer George Gershwin to fame with the premier of "Rhapsody in Blue".

The true king of jazz was Louis Armstrong, whose musical impact extended even beyond his melodic imagination (he invented the solo), his rhythmic genius (he taught the world to swing), his invention of scat singing, and his global impact. His beautiful tone, relaxed phrasing, fluid lines, and expressive style made his musical voice inextricable from his instrument. In short, it is not just beautiful trumpet playing you hear, it's *Louis Armstrong*.

Until Armstrong, most jazz soloists only made brief statements full of decorative embellishments, dramatic flourishes, or novelty effects. Armstrong made every note count and effectively used musical space to build his solos to a climax, akin to a writer placing the right word in a sentence to aesthetic effect. He did not separate serious music from humor, "Art" from joy. There was also always blues feeling in his solos, such as in the Hot Five's "Gut Bucket Blues". The song kicks off with a banjo solo and Armstrong cheers on each bandmember's solo (e.g., "whip that thing [piano], Miss Lil") before his twenty-second solo both swings and bends notes, with slurs analogous to a guitarist's slide (1:56-2:16).

Armstrong embodied the history of New Orleans music and made it global. His tone came from the cornetists and trumpeters of his childhood (e.g., Freddie Keppard, Joe Oliver), including their tricks, such as shaking the trumpet to create bent notes. From recording with blues singers Bessie Smith and Ethel Waters, he learned how to vocalize his sound. From his friendships with Bing Crosby and Hoagy Carmichael, he absorbed the musical structure of the standards from the Great American Songbook and became one of its finest interpreters. *(For more on Armstrong's vocal style, see the Chicago chapter).*

In the early 1920s, the best New Orleans musicians left their hometown for better economic opportunities, spreading the musical gospel to Paris (Bechet), California (Jelly Roll Morton), and Chicago (Armstrong, Oliver, Kid Ory, Johnny and Baby Dodds). As they traveled, they took all of its history along. Sidney Bechet said his grandparents heard a brand new set of sounds when the Civil War ended, loud and as-yet unformed, something they passed down to him as "emancipation music".

New Orleans, Then and Now

The polyphony, humor, and syncopated parade rhythms of New Orleans music echoes forward in jazz development to Charles Mingus' compositions, Arthur Blythe's tuba-powered ensembles, and drummer Ed Blackwell's symbiotic relationship with Ornette Coleman. To hear how the New Orleans sound infuses a broader jazz tradition, listen to drummer Jack DeJohnette's "New Orleans Strutt" (1984) or Henry Threadgill's "The Devil Is on the Loose and Dancin' With A Monkey" (1989).

Jazz remains a living tradition in clubs, on Sunday second-line parades, and in the city's high school marching bands. Jazz funerals are still held for the city's soldiers of music who carry its spirit of *surviving-in-style* through the streets. Musicians still play all night to honor a fallen fellow musician in the Treme, one of the nation's oldest communities of free people-of-color. When the brass band tradition nearly died out in the 1970s, Danny Barker revived it by organizing the Fairview Baptist Church band. It became a training ground for young musicians who revitalized the traditional marches with funk, soul, and hiphop: alumni include Wynton and Branford Marsalis, drummer Herlin Riley, trumpeter Leroy Jones, trombonist Lucien Barbarin, and members of the Dirty Dozen Brass Band.

New Orleans jazz is in all of the city's music, including soul, funk, and rock-and-roll. The architect of the Fats Domino sound was swing-era trumpeter and bandleader Dave Bartholomew. Born in 1918, Bartholomew grew up on second lines and learned trumpet from one of Louis Armstrong's teachers.

After World War II, he led the house swing band at the Dew Drop Inn —the city's most important Black club, akin to New York's Apollo Theater. Bartholomew co-wrote, arranged, and produced all of Fats Domino's hits such as "Ain't That a Shame", leading a crack band that included a trio of jazz saxophonists and innovative funk drummer Earl Palmer. These hits were recorded at Cosimo Matassa's legendary J&M Recording Studio, where Bartholomew's house band influenced the next generation of New Orleans musicians, including Allen Toussaint, Dr. John, and the Neville Brothers.

New Orleans musicians constantly revive jazz's first principles —personalized instrumental voices, infectious rhythmic grooves, innovative and powerful horn-playing. This is why the city's musicians were integral to jazz's neo-classical movement in the 1980s and the establishment of Jazz at Lincoln Center and its orchestra. Wynton Marsalis, Harry Connick, Jr., Terence Blanchard, Donald Harrison, Herlin Riley —all are New Orleans natives, raised in its musical traditions. Blanchard scores all of Spike Lee's films and composed the most evocative portrait of the Katrina experience, *Requiem*; Connick learned piano from the legendary pianist, James Booker. New Orleans still boasts a set of world-class jazz musicians: among them, trumpeter Nicholas Payton, clarinetist Evan Christopher, saxophonist Kidd Jordan, pianist Tom McDermott, alto saxophonist Aurora Nealand, and drummer Johnny Vidacovitch.

The affirming vitality of New Orleans music has again risen to national consciousness through Trombone Shorty, the Marsalis family, the HBO show Treme, and pianist/bandleader Jonathan Batiste on *The Late Show with Stephen Colbert*. On second lines, brass bands such as Rebirth and the Hot 8 still play the occasional jazz classic: I've heard Ellington's "It Don't Mean a Thing (If It Ain't Got That Swing")", Horace Silver's "Song of My Father", and the Dirty Dozen Brass Band's medley of "Stormy Monday" and "Blue Monk". This is the continuum of horn-powered New Orleans music on the streets within a broader national jazz tradition.

Finally, New Orleans jazz was the twentieth century's sound of freedom in France and much of Europe. The liberation of Paris from Nazi occupation had New Orleans music for its soundtrack. When French philosopher Simone de Beauvoir saw Louis Armstrong in Paris in 1946, she reported that his band made "the youth mad with enthusiasm", and called the concert "maybe the best thing I heard or saw in years". Jazz was, as well, the cry of youthful resistance against the Soviet Union in Eastern Europe, according to Czech novelist Josef Skvorecky —an existential affirmation through rhythmic propulsion and self-expression.

Beauvoir visited New Orleans in 1947 and experienced jazz on its home court. She described it as a new *kind* of art form: improvisatory, direct, self-excavating, in-the-moment. "Compared with art, poetry, and printed music, jazz has the privileged emotional impact of a communication that is immediate and fleeting", she observed, "like the very moments it transfigures". She resented the white Southern racist audiences at these clubs who treated these Black men as their servant entertainers playing happy-go-lucky music. She heard the exact opposite, the cry for individual freedom: "It's here in these modest clubs, among these unknown musicians … that jazz achieves its true dignity: there's no entertainment, no exhibitionism, no commercialism —for certain men, it's a way of life and a reason for being".

Jazz offers musicians a public artistic form and forum to speak in a *signature voice* and to make a statement *in-the-moment*. This is Bechet's freedom: each musician *speaks* and each supports the other, so you "get in for your own chance, freeing yourself". This is one key reason why jazz had immediate global popular appeal —and continues to appeal— to musicians and listeners around the world.

Chapter 2
Chicago: Jazz and the Great Migration

In 1922, Irish-American guitarist Eddie Condon walked into Lincoln Gardens, a new type of urban nightclub holding upwards of a thousand customers. King Oliver's Creole Jazz Band was on-stage and "the whole joint was rocking" and even "the tables, chairs, [and] walls moved with the rhythm". As Condon recalled it, "the trumpets, King and Louis [Armstrong] soared above everything else", and it seemed like "everything and everybody was moving, sliding, tapping out the rhythm, inhaling the smoke, swilling the gin". Within a few weeks, King Oliver started leaving a front row open for white apprentices, "a place near the band reserved for musicians who came to listen and to learn", Condon recalled, "and we sat there, stiff with education".

The major triad of Chicago jazz in the 1920s was *gangsters-nightclubs-jazz*. Gangsters built glamorous new venues, white Chicagoans learned jazz from its New Orleans artists, and the musicians shared ideas in nightclubs and at jam sessions. Jobs were plentiful since Prohibition created a different register of excitement and a new era of nightlife: with alcohol illegal, just getting a drink was a defiant act of rebellion. When Joe Oliver sent a train ticket to Armstrong, he joined the exodus to Chicago, along with Bechet and Jelly Roll Morton, drummers Zutty Singleton and Baby Dodds, trombonist Kid Ory and clarinetist Jimmie Noone.

Why did gangsters make jazz the cultural draw of these new clubs? "It got guts and it didn't make you slobber", one local gunman told Condon. Jazz fit Chicago like its overhead subways, a music for an industrial metropolis that sprung up over only two generations. Chicago was the nation's second-largest city, a magnet for immigrants and small-town Midwestern youth, an artistic center of literature and music. Jazz became faster, louder, and more organized in Chicago, reflecting a synthesis of an industrial Northern environment with the still-agrarian South.

Jazz also represented the hopes of the *Great Migration* with New Orleans musicians as its artistic leaders. Between 1910-1960, 70% of African-Americans left the neo-slavery of sharecropping and Southern terrorism for the factory jobs and relative freedom of industrial cities. Chicago was a major destination of the migration as it was home to a sizable Black middle-class and the nation's most influential Black weekly newspaper (*The Defender*). At smaller black nightclubs, the migrants were the principal audiences: white jazz musicians and fans were welcomed, if sometimes grudgingly.

Chicago's Black & Tan clubs were the first integrated public spaces in America and their interracial jam sessions were among the first of their kind. In jazz culture, everyone hung out on "The Stroll" —State St., the main drag— and white fans and musicians picked up African-American slang, style, and attitudes. Chicago's jazz scene reflected a set of better schools, access to the ballot, and vibrant political activism without violent reprisal. The South Side of Chicago was Harlem's equal as a capital of Black America and its musical culture analogous to the more literary Harlem Renaissance.

Yet the city was strictly segregated until the 1960s and Blacks experienced considerable oppression. Jazz in Chicago was art *and* protest, individual quest and social statement, musical declarations of freedom and celebrations of group survival. It can be heard in the hard, funky, earthy Chicago saxophone style of the 1950s. *As* playwright and activist Lorraine Hansberry wrote of her hometown: "Our South Side is a place apart. My people are poor, and they are tired, and they are determined to live. Each piece of our living is a protest".

Chicago has been home to three key phases of jazz developments: its transformation of New Orleans jazz in the 1920s; the collective improvisation of the 1960s; the avant-garde scene of the 1990s. All three periods are linked by the Great Migration. The children of the Migration's first wave came of age with an aesthetic urge towards musical freedom: they founded the Association for the Advancement of Creative Musicians (AACM), a key jazz institution, and formed its key unit, the Art Ensemble of Chicago. The AACM's legacy lingered into the 1990s, when a younger multi-ethnic generation stirred in punk, rock, funk, and ethnic rhythms to create this century's most vital avant-garde scene.

The 1920s: White Apprentices, Black Masters

Chicago's first phase shaped jazz in several ways. The rhythmic section of banjo and tuba was replaced by guitar and upright bass, creating a more fluid rhythm. More rhythmic layers were needed to reflect the industrial soundscape: the modern drum set emerged with its bass, tom-tom, high-hat, snare, and cymbals; the "hot" two-beat rhythm (2/4) morphed slowly into the even 4/4 rhythm. Musicians moved away from collective improvisation with fixed horn sections, freeing up more solo space. The tenor saxophone was the rising sound: in New York, Coleman Hawkins created its heavy, rhapsodic sound but an influential lighter approach came through Chicago's Bud Freeman].

Urban Industrial Rhythms

At the end of World War I in 1918, white New Orleans clarinetist Leon Roppolo and trombonist George Brunies moved to Chicago and formed the New Orleans Rhythm Kings. The band's biggest fans were a group of Chicago teenagers known as the Austin High (School) Gang, who practiced their songs all day, much like garage bands would later with rock-and-roll. But the first time the Austin High Gang heard King Oliver and Armstrong, they realized, *oh, so here are the true creators and geniuses of this modern music.* Black and Tans such as Lincoln Gardens and the Grand Terrace were sites of cultural transmission.

Consider these young white Chicagoans as the first *hipsters,* a slang word that for two generations meant *an aficionado of jazz.* Many left memoirs of their jazz revelations, such as Jewish-American clarinetist Mezz Mezzrow's *Really the Blues* (1946). Mezzrow apprenticed to Bechet for his sound, Armstrong as the scene's genius, and drummer Zutty Singleton for rhythmic guidance. He was the first white writer to understand jazz as a subversive existential response to oppression: "The colored people, fresh up out of 300 years of slavery, still the despised pariahs of the country in spite of their 'liberation'... had roared out a revolutionary new music to shout that message to the world". He recognized the music as an affirmative repudiation of racism and depression: "It was a defiance of the undertaker. It was a refusal to go under, a stubborn hanging-on, a shout of praise to the circulatory system... Praise be the almighty pulse! Ain't nobody going to wash us away". To Mezzrow, jazz's joyful noise was the flip side of the Delta blues: "what New Orleans was really saying was a celebration of life, of breathing, of muscle-flexing in spite of everything the world might do to you".

White Midwestern boys thrilled to jazz within a 500-mile radius of Chicago: many heard the music on the steamboats that came up the Mississippi River carrying New Orleans' best musicians. The brilliant, dreamy trumpeter Leon "Bix" Beiderbecke hung around the harbor in his hometown of Davenport, Iowa, and soon converted Indiana ragtime pianist Hoagy Carmichael. Bix was a young idol of white musicians and college youth: he had a soft, romantic sound incongruous with his legendary drunkenness. Carmichael wrote several jazz standards and he was Armstrong's favorite songwriter for standards such as "Skylark", "Stardust", "Am I Blue", and "Georgia On My Mind". Bix and Carmichael were regulars on the Chicago scene until hired together by Paul Whiteman.

Bix and Carmichael created something akin to *riverboat jazz*, a lighter, less edgy variant of New Orleans music. Listen to "Riverboat Shuffle" by The Wolverines, with its bright opening theme, lighter rhythmic flow, quick riffs, jerky stops and starts, and resonant banjo strumming. The ensemble revs like an engine for a full minute then falls back to let Bix take a long, forty-second solo. Bix's burnished tone and understated harmonic invention display a new trumpet voice, as does his alternation of quick riffs and silences. The band then replays the theme (1:34-1:52) to set up a clarinet solo that begins by ascending the scale and pushes the song's tempo. The song's final phase features *call-and-response* between Bix and the ensemble, followed by a short ride-out chorus that seems to merrily say, "and that's that!"

Two major new musicians pushed Armstrong to new heights, pianists Earl Hines and Lil Hardin. Hardin was a classically-trained college graduate from Memphis who accompanied blues and vaudeville singers before joining King Oliver's band. She encouraged Armstrong to leave Oliver, organized his first recording unit —Louis Armstrong's Hot Five— then married him. Listen to Hardin set up the band on the scat classic, "Heebie Jeebies", then swing her own band in "Come Back, Sweet Papa" (1925). When the marriage broke up, Hardin led a band at the Dreamland Café, then moved to California.

Earl Hines arrived from Pittsburgh with a virtuosic, trumpet-style fluidity on the piano. Hines was the pianist in Armstrong's Hot Seven but it is in their famous duet —"Weather Bird"— that we can hear the quantum development of jazz in just a decade. Trumpet and piano establish an easy, rolling foundation, then each launches into a breakthrough solo. Their intuition is marvelous as they delight in the fast-paced musical intuition of fingers that match their quick minds —when either pauses, the other quickly jumps in with a short, dramatic riff or figure. This is a championship match rendered as conversation between artistic equals.

Hines led an influential big band heard by half the country on its weekly radio broadcast, "Live from the Grand Terrace". Listeners might hear "Chicago Rhythm", with its light theme that deepens as the band thickens with propulsion and industrial density underneath the call-and-response with the soloists. Hines' biggest hit was "Rosetta", a jazz standard that sets a leisurely Sunday-afternoon mood. There a familiar New Orleans trumpet voice to bring it to life, a scatted vocal that echoes the theme, and then Hines provides the climax (@ 1:52) with a crisp 30-second solo.

The Austin High Gang went to see everyone and approached jazz as devotees to a new art form —in fact, as the vibrant, individualist, emerging spirit of America itself. Led by their intellectual alto saxophonist, Frank Teschemacher, and the savvy white drummer Davey Tough, they played at roadhouses, frat parties, summer resorts, and late-night jam sessions. Listen to the uptempo "I've Found A New Baby" (1928) for the clarity of each musician's personality and rhythmic attunement.

Joel Dinerstein

QIJ - Chicago

Created by Joel Dinerstein · 14 songs, 1 hr 17 min

PLAY (···)

FOLLOWERS 0

Download ⊙

TITLE	ARTIST	ALBUM	📅	
Riverboat Shuffle	Bix Beiderbecke	The Golden Age Of Bix ...	2019-02-05	3:12
Oh! You Sweet Thing	Earl Hines & His Orche...	Classic Earl Hines Sessi...	2019-04-15	2:55
Weather Bird	Louis Armstrong; Earl ...	Louis Armstrong: Portr...	2019-04-03	2:42
Blue Again	Louis Armstrong	Volume 7 You're Drivin...	2020-04-22	3:11
A Slick Chick (On The Mellow Side) - Single Ve...	Dinah Washington, Tab...	Queen: The Music Of D...	2019-04-29	2:40
I Cried for You	Johnny Griffin, Wilbur...	The Chicago Sound	2019-05-09	3:37
Evil Eye - Rudy Van Gelder 24Bit Mastering	Clifford Jordan, John ...	Blowing In From Chicago	2019-02-18	5:15
Soft Talk	Sun Ra	Supersonic Jazz	2019-06-03	2:41
The First Time Ever I Saw Your Face	Von Freeman	Don' It Right Now	2019-05-02	4:37
Promenade: Cote Bamako I	Art Ensemble Of Chica...	Urban Bushmen	2019-02-17	4:14
From the River to the Ocean	Fred Anderson, Hamid ...	From the River to the C...	2019-05-08	13:36
20th Century Myth	DKV Trio	Latitude	2019-05-08	17:53

3. Dinerstein's Chicago playlist.

Chicago's first phase of jazz ended due to the efforts of political reform organizations. The election of a new mayor in 1928 resulted in the political harassment of nightclubs and African-American bandleaders, often triggered by white resentment of the competition. By 1930, most white Chicagoans had moved to New York and many Black musicians moved to Los Angeles, including Armstrong and Morton. The Earl Hines Orchestra held on at the Grand Terrace through World War II with a weekly radio broadcast that influenced jazz musicians from Michigan to New Mexico.

Of the New Orleans cohort, Jimmie Noone's Apex Club Orchestra played for the longest on the South Side: it was a so-called "sweet" band, a term that referred to smoothing out the syncopation and emphasizing the melody (as on "After You've Gone"). Noone's clarinet style influenced a young Benny Goodman, later the "King of Swing" in the big band era. Clarinetist Johnny Dodds had a band with his brother, drummer Baby Dodds, who was one model for Goodman's drummer, Gene Krupa, a jazz icon and teen idol of the big band era. Krupa's featured singer was Anita O'Day, a Chicago jazz vocalist whose influence rivaled Billie Holiday's in the 1950s. O'Day's iconic version of "Sweet Georgia Brown" at the Newport Jazz Festival in 1960 can be heard on the wonderful time-capsule documentary, *Jazz On a Summer's Day.*

Chicago jazz musicians were the first artists to acknowledge their use of marijuana for its relaxed vibe and heightened musical appreciation. Marijuana smokers were called *vipers* and joints were called *muggles*, the hip jazz slang represented by Armstrong's "Muggles" (1928) and Fats Waller's "Viper's Drag" (1929). Mezzrow is now best remembered as Armstrong's pot dealer and the latter called his joints "mezz" and "mezzeolas". Gene Krupa, a true Chicago drummer, became national news when busted for marijuana possession in 1946.

Here is a piece of jazz lore that captures this era's combination of rebellion, drugs, jazz, and race. In 1926, pianist Fats Waller was playing the whites-only College Inn when two men stuck a gun in his ribcage and dragged him blindfolded to a limousine; Waller thought he was going to be killed. Soon enough, he was shoved down at a piano and opened his eyes to a roomful of gangsters —it was Al Capone's birthday and his men brought the boss his favorite pianist as a birthday present! Waller played as if his life was at stake —it might have been— but Capone loved his present and the music. The gangster boss and virtuoso pianist spent the next three days drinking and carousing, at which point Capone stuffed a few thousand bucks in Waller's pocket and dropped him back at his hotel. This story is like a one-reel silent film of Jim Crow Chicago.

Interlude: Louis Armstrong Invents the American Vocal Style

Louis Armstrong first took up singing in Chicago with a voice that was more a crooning baritone than his later trademark gravelly voice —with it, he created a pop revolution. Armstrong altered melody lines to give songs catchier rhythms; he changed lyrics to suit his voice and the song's message. His phrasing on trumpet influenced his vocal phrasing (and vice-versa) while his conversational vocal style helped bring an end to an age of big voices and strict enunciation.

Armstrong transformed every song into an artful, personalized act with his expressive, unmistakable voice. Before him, there were proper ways of singing requiring a "good voice"; after him, infusing one's personality became the American vocal style. His achievement was partly based on recognizing that the microphone —first used in recording in 1925— made possible a new kind of intimate singing. There was also his unique synthesis of vocal traditions: for phrasing and intonation, he drew on Irish tenors such as John McCormick, opera singers such as Enrico Caruso, blues singers such as Bessie Smith, and Yiddish singers he heard while living with a New Orleans Jewish family (the Karnofskys).

Armstrong was the first Black man to croon romantic songs into America's white pop imagination. "Blue Again" is an ironically triumphant march about romantic rejection: he is "blue again" yet the tone of his vocal is all hope and resilience, while his solo drives the band to a victorious ending crescendo. In "Walkin' My Baby Back Home", his opening trumpet solo balances confidence, romance, and swing while the horn section responds with startling warmth, laying down a red carpet of ethnic pride. Armstrong inscribed his own experience into American music by interpreting classics such as "When Your Lover Has Gone", "I Surrender Dear", and "Lazy River". On "Just A Gigolo", he rhymes his occupation ("just a gigolo") with "just a *jig-I-know*", a racial epithet that projects his awareness of how white Americans think of his people.

On his pop-jazz songs in particular, you can hear that Armstrong's having a ball. When the band's energy slackens for a moment during "You're Driving Me Crazy", he roars out, "Swing, *swing* you dogs", then his trumpet solo shows the ensemble how it's done. On "Up A Lazy River", he sighs a joyful "*Yeaaah*" upon hearing the sweet blend of the horn section, then scats a few phrases and says, as if to himself, "*Boy, if I ain't riffing this evening!*" At the beginning of "Chinatown, My Chinatown", he says, as if describing jazz conversation, "we are going to have a little argument between the saxophone and the trumpet", then as he trades riffs, he interjects, "It looks like they're after me!"

Novelist Ralph Ellison considered Armstrong a trickster figure, due to his deft mixture of encoded resistance (for black listeners) and racial deference (laughing to stay employed). Armstrong gave a command performance to the King and Queen of England in 1932 and just before singing the humorous revenge fantasy, "I'll Be Glad When You're Dead, You Rascal You", he caught the King's eye and said, "This one's for you, Rex". Wishing any king dead in his presence is a bold, defiant, comic move, but this was part-and-parcel of Armstrong's appeal. Yet on "Little Joe", Armstrong offers his love to a little boy as a shield against racism: "Even though the white folks/ they think nothing of you, / they always send you away", remember, he sings, "you're my little pride and joy".

Bing Crosby, the world's most successful pop singer from 1900-1950, adapted Armstrong's innovations —swing, intimacy, humor, surprise— into his own style. The key was to make singing seem as natural as breathing, as easy as conversation, as intimate as talking with a friend. At a tribute for songwriter Hoagy Carmichael, Bing Crosby turned to him and sang, "Do you realize that the greatest pop singer is Louis Armstrong?" The three were good friends and mutually influenced jazz for two generations.

When bebop transformed jazz in the 1940s, Armstrong's star power remained but vocals became secondary and the saxophone eclipsed the trumpet as the voice of change. Yet his influence on vocalists remained strong, from Frank Sinatra to Billie Holiday, from Ella Fitzgerald to Sarah Vaughan and even Chuck Berry. Billie Holiday always said that she tried to combine Armstrong's swing with Bessie

Smith's emotional power: "I always wanted Bessie's big sound and Pops' *feeling*". Musicologist Gunther Schuller believes Armstrong "added a new school or technique of singing to Western music".

The Chicago Saxophone Sound, 1940-1965

Out of the eclectic offerings of the South Side music scene came the distinctive quality of postwar Chicago jazz. Nightclubs featured small-combo bands with horns, such as Big Bill Broonzy's jazzed-up Delta-blues or Dinah Washington's jazzy R&B singles such as "Slick Chick on the Mellow Side". Muddy Waters, Howlin' Wolf, and other Delta musicians moved up in the 1950s and created the Chicago blues. To bassist Malachi Favors of the AACM, the South Side was then "the greatest entertainment section in the world. Even as New York's bebop revolution transformed jazz into a music where the solo became the focus of jazz *(see chapter four),* Chicago nurtured its own sound and scene at jam sessions.

Most jam-session leaders were tenor saxophonists and wore their civic and aesthetic pride on their album sleeves: Johnny Griffin's *The Chicago Sound* (1957), Clifford Jordan and John Gilmore, *Blowing in from Chicago* (1957), Eddie Harris, *Exodus to Jazz* (1961). All were known for "blowing hard" with a rough, earthy sound and passionate soloing. Jordan and Gilmore swing the mid-tempo "Blue Lights" to evoke bar-hopping with its atmospheric late night theme: the first solo belongs to Gilmore's aggressive bebop style, the second to Jordan's bluesy bounce. Yet all were equally adept at ballads, as Harris shows with his elegant rendering of "Theme from *Exodus*" and the yearning of "Alicia".

On *The Chicago Sound*, Griffin was joined by jam session veterans bassist Wilbur Ware and pianist Junior Mance. "I Cried For You" is a mid-tempo ballad with the Chicago difference: Griffin swings warmly for the first half of a two-minute solo then hits a strident descending riff (@ 1:16) and starts blowing that fast, earthy, Chicago style. Mance's piano enters with a few strong blues chords and stray tinkling phrases that moderate Griffin's intensity. On "31ST and State" —a famous South Side intersection— Ware begins with a bluesy, easy-rolling 90-second bass solo until Griffin's tenor struts in like a man hitting the street with swag and purpose. Mance's solo adds a third personality, supportive rather than showy. Now we have three distinctive, individual jazz voices hanging out and swapping stories on the corner.

John Gilmore was searching for new musical directions and found it with the Sun Ra Arkestra, an Afrofuturist big band founded in Chicago. On the Arkestra's first album (*Super-Sonic Jazz*, 1957), compositions such as "Kingdom of Not" feature an evocative mix of urban, atmospheric and futuristic rhythms. Pianist Herman "Sonny" Blount of

Birmingham, Alabama, moved to Chicago and had a vision to "tune up the world" in 1952. He changed his name to Sun Ra, then drew on Egyptian mythological motifs for the Arkestra's costumes, theatricality, innovative compositions, and performative chants. Over four prolific decades, Sun Ra always claimed he was from Saturn and that his band's music was for "traveling the spaceways" —with Gilmore by his side as his primary soloist.

Perhaps the quintessential Chicago saxophonist was Von Freeman —an iconoclast and a one-man jazz institution who embodied a century of Chicago jazz. Born in 1923, Freeman went to DuSable High School and studied under legendary music teacher Captain Walter Dyett. His father was a policeman and amateur trombonist in the 1920s: Armstrong, Earl Hines, and Fats Waller were regular visitors to his home. Freeman played in a variety of bands in the 1950s —blues bands, bebop combos, Chicago-style jazz, Sun Ra's Arkestra— but did not record until 1972's *Doin' It Right Now*. Then nearly fifty, all Chicago's musical streams seemed to mesh in his funky, ribald, propulsive sound: R&B honking, down home blues, bebop's harmonic complexity, avant-garde breathing techniques. On "First Time Ever I Saw His Face", he transforms the hit ballad with a knowing, lyrical narration by turns romantic, meditative, and forceful. When the piano cascades in, the rhythm section maintains an exemplary equilibrium, allowing for a piano-and-saxophone duet in the final minute.

In 1980, Von Freeman began a legendary 30-year residency on Tuesday nights at a remote South Side bar, the New Apartment Lounge. The altoist Steve Coleman recalled Von Freeman's public mentorship:

There was a guy called Von Freeman in Chicago where I grew up. He didn't formally give me lessons, but he was like a mentor. Watching him year after year changed my life. I would make private recordings and [when] I played them back later, there was so much to get: *the rhythm, the way it flowed, melody, harmony, saxophone stuff like fingering and breathing* —there's so much you're getting all at once when you see somebody live. I won't say that I didn't try to study with Von —but he said, 'No —I don't teach'.

In the 1990s, the young saxophonist Matana Roberts frequented Freeman's weekly gig and learned "to understand the history of the music" and how to put "her own personal stamp" on jazz. This led directly to *The Chicago Project* (2008), her own album in the city's jazz tradition. In 2002, Chicago renamed the New Apartment's block "Von Freeman Way".

The AACM's Quest for Total Musical Freedom

The children of the Great Migration were young adults during the civil rights movement and their artistic aims reflected its political objectives to unshackle their creativity. Founded in 1965, the

Association for the Advancement of Creative Musicians took as its charter the pursuit of original improvised music within a collective unit. The AACM created an experimental jazz built on collective spontaneity, musical space, implicit rhythms, and new sounds. One origin of its principles came from the composition workshops of pianist Muhal Richard Abrams: he required musicians to compose from day one, forcing them to develop original and individual ideas. One day Roscoe Mitchell and bassist Malachi Favors brought their friend, Joseph Jarman, to the workshop and AACM's showcase unit was born: the Art Ensemble of Chicago.

The Art Ensemble took the stage in costumes and face paint, improvising resonant moments fueled by African percussion, random noises, ethnic traditions, and avant-garde classical music. It was steeped in a guerrilla theater aesthetic of the 1960s and brought evocations of shamanistic musical practice into jazz. The Art Ensemble pushed the idea of what constituted music in dynamic, playful, abrasive, and surprising ways. Structures were loose and free —without melody, standard harmony, or a regular beat. Jarman played atonal dissonant solos, alternating between shrieks and bellows. He had a table of so-called "little instruments" —toys, bells, found objects, hand percussion— that expanded the sonic palette of jazz. The Art Ensemble explored how pure sound resonates into silence and bounces off everything, including their excited Black audiences on the South Side.

AACM artists yoked together sounds and approaches from all over the world. "We play the blues, we play jazz, rock, Spanish music, gypsy, African, contemporary European music", Jarman once said, "we create sounds, period". Anthony Braxton combined a Delta blues aesthetic with the approaches of classical composers Arnold Schoenberg, John Cage, and Karl Stockhausen; Jarman was influenced by African ballet, Ornette Coleman's free jazz, and hippie culture; Roscoe Mitchell studied under both free jazz saxophonist Albert Ayler and a clarinetist of the Heidelberg Symphony; Famadou Don Moye grew up on gospel and bebop, but playing with African drummers in Paris transformed his approach.

Here are two analyses of key performances of the Art Ensemble. Each may sound like a musical free-for-all but better to think of it as music for cerebral surfing. Assume and impose nothing, just ride the waves of sound.

"Promenade: Cote Bamako II" is named for the capital of Mali and evokes the sense of arriving at the capital from a small village. It begins with a proclamation by drum cymbal, followed by African hand percussion that skitters along like musical pebbles, and a struck Chinese gong. Lester Bowie's trumpet blows a clarion call as if an elephant has arrived (00:43) —then Jarman's alto saxophone hoots like an owl, and musical snakes rustle along from every instrument for thirty seconds. A quiet section then evokes midday heat on the savannah until a whistle is blown, as if calling the environment itself to order. Gongs and larger African drums now enter with great power to play the composition's first repetitive rhythmic pattern. We now enter the city as a group, the whistle leading, the congas guiding our musical steps, the rhythm increasing —there is a loud, resonant vocal call and we have arrived. It is the opening track of a live album, *Urban Bushmen.*

Jarman's "Fanfare for the Warriors" is a more *outside* composition —the term for an aesthetic akin to controlled chaos. There is an angular opening theme and then the horns unite, separate, and reunite for a full minute —then the song *implodes* into a wild succession of independent calls, shouts, and polyphony. Each player improvises according to his musical soundworld as the other members of the ensemble listen and respond. It is an impressive cacophony of engaged voices: horns squawk, percussion crackles, bells shimmer, the piano scatters riffs like lizards. Jarman's alto screeches into the higher register as if trying to reach the gods while Roscoe Mitchell's tenor blasts urban power. And when you least expect it, the horns hit a unifying riff to call everyone together (@ 5:58): Bowie's trumpet mutters into a corner, trailing off, his rant unfinished; the piano moves into the center with calming, meditative waves of sound. Over the final two minutes the music quiets: each musician finishes his statement and a final percussive splash ends the fanfare. This is musical catharsis: the listener feels as if they have been through a dynamic experience, whether cleansed, turned-on, or offended.

AACM musicians were acclaimed first by music critics in Paris when they moved there as a group in 1969. European critics understood the Art Ensemble's music as a synthesis of avant-garde classical music, African-American musical forms, mathematical structures, jazz practices, ethnic rhythms, and pure sound. Their album titles indicate this dynamic mix: Muhal Richard Abrams, *1-OQA+19*, Anthony Braxton's *Creative Orchestra Music*, Henry Threadgill's *Just the Facts and Pass the Bucket*, the Art Ensemble's *Message To Our Folks*. When the Art Ensemble moved to New York in the 1970s, their musical influence permeated all of global music. The Art Ensemble modeled first, how improvising musicians *listen to each other* to create a tapestry of sound without a leader, and second, how to listen to rhythmic textures without a melody.

Chicago's Ongoing Avant-Garde: 1990-2020

Alone amongst the original AACM members, tenor saxophonist Fred Anderson remained in Chicago after the 1960s. He midwifed the next avant-garde scene by carrying on AACM's principles at his nightclub, The Velvet Lounge, through his generosity, mentorship, civic boosterism, and sheer force of personality. Anderson's jazz life runs parallel to Von Freeman's: his tenor sound was earthy and urgent, his jam sessions had global reach, he recorded late in life. A new era of Chicago jazz began in the 1990s —with the arrival of saxophonist Ken Vandermark, with the opening of a key second club, The Empty Bottle, and with younger musicians conditioned by punk, metal, and dissonance. Both Anderson and Vandermark record often with Hamid Drake, the most creative and influential drummer of the past generation.

Anderson and Drake are musical soulmates who grew up a generation apart in Monroe, Louisiana, and their shared background fuels *From the River to the Ocean* (2010), one of the great jazz albums of this century. It features three compositions of more than thirteen minutes, each grounded in a roiling, buoyant groove created by two bassists. "Strut Time" is twenty-one minutes of assertive, headstrong funky street-walking: Anderson's Chicago tenor struts on a groovy church bed of organ, guitar, and drums, with a cello tossing in phrases that create dissonance. "Planet E" begins with Anderson making a saxophone proclamation that sounds like a call to action: guitarist Jeff Parker's solo follows as if guiding the listeners down to the ship to start the journey. Drake supports and challenges each soloist while maintaining the groove's dynamic equilibrium; he quiets only when Anderson steps up to speak his piece. A similar mood of amphibious wandering carries the title track: it evokes a solitary figure back at home, sitting down by the ocean pondering the history and future of his people. On "Sakti/Shiva", the final track, Anderson's short phrases project solidity, place, poise, and equilibrium, a momentary stasis within the planet's ocean of sound. The title suggests the unity of divine male and female energies in the Hindu pantheon and the piece brings this epic journey home.

Ken Vandermark grew up in the Boston area and became a catalyst for the Chicago scene upon arrival, in particular through his Vandermark 5 and later with the DKV Trio, featuring Hamid Drake and bassist Kent Kessler. The DKV Trio combines ethnic soundings from various cultural traditions (Greek, Middle Eastern, Japanese, Brazilian) with African-American funk and blues grafted onto the rhythmic explorations of Steve Reich and Philip Glass. Vandermark calls his compositions "song structures".

On the DKV Trio's *Latitude 41.88* (2017), three long tracks integrate solos into a heady percussive stew. Drake opens "20th Century Myth" with a five-minute drum solo that alternates near-vocal phrases on the tablas with martial rhythms and whispered shimmerings. Vandermark enters with quiet, measured phrases and Kessler's bowed bass adds a deep, low undercurrent. His honk signals a new movement and, after a minute, the trio locks into a propulsive groove with that rough, earthy Chicago sound but it also sounds Indian, Mississippian, Central African. This groove engages the listener's guts and hips for a while then rolls into collective deep blues wailing —it works both as the trio's protest against the city's intractable problems and as a call to action. For the last two minutes Vandermark plays short phrases within an octave that descends into the final elegiac notes of meditation on "Latitude 41.88" —the cartographic location of Chicago.

Chicago Jazz Keeps On Keepin' On

In 1934, *Downbeat* was founded in Chicago, the first important jazz magazine: within five years its circulation soared to 80,000, a sign of jazz's arrival as the national music. Chicago's 1920s paved the road to the big-band era, which influenced the global soundscape for a generation. White Chicagoans Benny Goodman and Gene Krupa became iconic bandleaders of World War II while Armstrong and Earl Hines led nationally-renowned big bands. Eddie Condon opened "Condon's" in Greenwich Village then moved it to New York's "swing street", West 52nd Street. In effect, the white Chicagoans became stalwart jazz traditionalists.

Incredibly, the atmosphere of Prohibition-era Chicago can still be found at the Green Mill, a beautiful, well-preserved club —where people still dance to jazz, where a plaque designates Al Capone's booth, where the triad of jazz-gangsters-speakeasy still hangs in the now-smokeless room. The club is no museum piece, but instead represents a convergence of the city's history. There is live jazz every night across many genres. The club's legendary Sunday afternoon jam sessions nurtures its avant-garde scene, including jazz electronica units such as the Exploding Star Orchestra or the Chicago Underground Duo.

The jazz of the Great Migration and that of their children were sonic opposites. The music of the 1920s was for social dance, the AACM's music was for concerts. Chicago jazz was organized through a rhythmic center and a melodic theme; AACM jazz was de-centered, dissonant, and marked by musical space. In 1920s jazz, there was usually one main soloist in the band; by the 1970s, musicians improvised simultaneously in collective composition. Two concepts unify the movements: improvisation and *freedom-through-music.* In the half-century from 1920-1970, jazz went from music for social dance to avant-garde art music; from 1970-2020, jazz absorbed global rhythms and classical music.

There is an annual Chicago Jazz Festival that is unusual in three ways: it's free, it remains connected to the South Side's Black community, and it features a tribute to a hometown jazz hero (e.g., Von Freeman, the Art Ensemble). The festival represents jazz as it reflects the multi-faceted creativity of its jazz generations.

Chapter 3

Kansas City: Swinging Into the Future, 1923-1943

New York's Fletcher Henderson Orchestra arrived in Kansas City on tour in 1935 as the nation's most influential and polished big band. The band's premier soloist, Coleman Hawkins, had mapped the tenor saxophone as a brand new instrument and wore this mastery with a certain aristocratic dignity. After the gig, Hawkins went to the Cherry Blossom club to watch the local musicians jam and a friend was shocked when Hawkins took the stage. Apparently, Hawkins thought the local musicians worthy of being vanquished! Instead he wound up in the musical battle of his life, having stumbled unknowingly into the nation's most vital and competitive jazz scene.

That night, in the most famous jam session in jazz history, Hawkins was sorely tested by three of jazz's future legends: Lester Young, Ben Webster, and Herschel Evans, all three then unrecorded and all-but- unknown. At 3am, Webster yelled up to the apartment window of pianist Mary Lou Williams: "Get up, pussycat, we're jammin' and all the pianists are tired out now. Hawkins has got his shirt off and is still blowing". She took over on piano and the battle went on until dawn. Legend has it that Hawkins burned out his engine driving 250 miles over rocky roads to make the Henderson band's next gig in St. Louis. Six short years later, Lester Young was the genius soloist of the Count Basie Orchestra, Herschel Evans was his foil, and Ben Webster was a driving force of the Duke Ellington Orchestra in the peak years of the two best big bands in jazz history.

Kansas City was the Las Vegas of the 1930s. "If you want to see some sin, forget Paris and go to Kansas City", one journalist wrote during Prohibition, referring to the city's all-night entertainment and near-naked waitresses. The city was a wide-open bazaar of gambling, alcohol, and prostitution under Mayor Tom Pendergast: he ran the political machine and (not coincidentally) was the city's main liquor distributor. There were rich cattlemen at the gritty Reno Club, a vibrant white middle-class dancing at the Pla-Mor ballroom, and working-class Blacks enjoying Joe Turner's raucous blues at the Sunset Club. Band gigs often went from nine-to-five —*9pm to 5am*— followed by jam sessions until noon.

Kansas City was an isolated metropolis, a frontier oasis, and the western terminus of the railroad. Since most national tours of "Eastern bands" and New York theater shows ended there, musicians kept up with jazz trends, new cosmopolitan dances, and the national entertainment scene. Charlie Parker, Ben Webster, Bennie Moten, and Big Joe Turner were the city's native sons. Parker grew up in the city's jam-session culture, a key foundation of his musical ingenuity in the creation of bebop after moving to New York in 1941.

When pianist Mary Lou Williams arrived from Pittsburgh in 1929, she found "fifty or more cabarets rocking" in the entertainment district. "The town was wide open for drinking, gambling and pretty much every form of vice", she recalled. "Naturally, work was plentiful for musicians". Williams quickly became the pianist/arranger for Andy Kirk's 12 Clouds of Joy and soon she was "The Lady Who Swings the Band": *when you hear the saxes ride/ who's the reason why they glide? It's the lady who swings the band!*

Of equal importance, Kansas City was the epicenter of a network of competitive "territory bands", none more feared than the Oklahoma City Blue Devils, the region's fiercest live group. Territory bands ranged from Dallas to the Dakotas, from Arkansas to Albuquerque, and included such legendary units as St. Louis's Jeter-Pillars Orchestra and Dallas's Alphonse Trent Band. When bands came to Kansas City, drummer Jo Jones said there was so much music in town that people *"walked* in time ... in *swing*-time".

Kansas City was a music workshop from which an all-star unit —the Count Basie Orchestra— swept into national prominence with an influential hard-swinging style. The band's loosely tight groove was at-once relaxed and propulsive: jazz theorist Albert Murray called it "the velocity of celebration". When the Basie band moved to New York in 1937, its musicians transformed the city's jazz culture with its jam-session zeal, rhythmic power, and blues-based solos. They brought a new idea of the jazz solo to New York —"to tell a story"— and riff-style arrangements more conducive to dancing. KC's vocalists were equally original: Jimmy Rushing, Big Joe Turner, Billie Holiday, and Julia Lee blended jazz, blues, and Tin Pan Alley pop into modern, influential vocal styles.

Kansas City was a short, transformational era of jazz history, essential and little-known, a missing key to the evolution of the blues and swing *within* jazz. Whether called "Kansas City swing" or "the Southwestern swing style", it revolutionized nearly *all* American music. Kansas City gave birth to Charlie Parker's bebop revolution, Billie Holiday's artistry, the lyricism of Lester Young and Ben Webster, the first electric guitar solos, and even rock-and-roll.

Homegrown Blues: Big Joe Turner and Bennie Moten

KC natives Bennie Moten (b. 1894) and Joe Turner (b. 1911) built on the city's strong blues and ragtime foundations to become the cornerstones of the legendary district around 18th and Vine. The city's Black community began as an early out-migration from the South to escape the terrorism of the Ku Klux Klan. Known as the Exodusters, this working-class community supported a vibrant music scene well before World War I. Moten built the city's best big band as a ragtime pianist and was admired for his fairness and leadership. Turner started singing on the streets as a twelve-year-old kid and became the district's blues-belting heart.

Bennie Moten took lessons in succession from his mother, a classical pianist, and then a ragtime student of Scott Joplin's. At 21, he freelanced for a year in the cabarets and formed his first band: The BB & D Quartet, a combo that drew two thousand dancers to its debut at the Labor Temple, a marker of the nation's public dance culture. An ambitious, organized businessman, Moten added strong soloists and established social connections on both sides of the color line. He developed the Paseo Dancing Academy into a major venue, yet even there, the Thamon Hayes Band soundly defeated him in the annual battle of the bands. In 1923, Moten's band became the first black band to broadcast on local radio (WHB) and they were soon backing up blues vocalists on recordings.

That same year, 12-year-old Joe Turner began accompanying a blind blues guitarist through the streets and in restaurants, first passing the tin cup and soon enough, singing along. Turner was steeped in the blues at home —singing to Bessie Smith and Ethel Waters records— and learned new songs from his uncles. At 16, Turner had a thunderous, expressive voice and could settle into any guitarist's groove, improvising several verses at a time. Musicians at the Backbiters Club once stole the mike while he was on break but Turner did not need amplification and just belted it out. He soon teamed up with pianist Pete Johnson and they became the soundtrack of the Sunset Club.

Moten's musicians often came by the Sunset to play an impromptu set and pass the hat for extra money. Late nights everyone wound up there: dancers, hustlers, musicians, actors, comedians. "Everybody up there was wonderful, everybody from the theatre [companies] would come by and they'd jam", recalled Cliff Leeman, a white swing drummer stranded in Kansas City. As a singing bartender, Turner would play a set with Johnson then walk out and sing in the street in an apron, wiping dishes, and "call his children home", the same phrase Buddy Bolden once used in New Orleans.

Moten's band was the city's best but his nemesis was the Oklahoma City Blue Devils. Run by bassist

Walter Page, the Blue Devils swung so hard "they didn't even need the drummer", arranger Jesse Stone once said. When the Great Depression hit and gigs dried up, Moten began poaching Page's best musicians until, by 1932, the two bands had effectively merged. Moten hired pianist Bill Basie, vocalist Jimmy Rushing, trumpeter Oran (Hot Lips) Page, saxophonists Buster Smith and Lester Young, trombonist/arranger Eddie Durham, and finally even Page himself.

This 1932 version of Moten's band captured the city's new sound with "Moten Swing" (1932) and here is its musical drama. The song opens with a self-assured rolling piano riff when suddenly the high-pitched trumpet section enters shouting (@ 00:18) —the saxophone section coolly responds then drops out, leaving the piano trio. The sax section then plays a fragment of the melody (@ 00:38) leading into a short guitar solo that sets up a new riff by the trombone section; the alto sax challenges, creating infectious call-and-response (1:35). A trumpet rides in with the rhythm section (@1:56), then enjoys a quick exchange with the saxophone before vaulting into the upper register. The low hum of the sax section is offset by this trumpet cry, creating a satisfying contrast. The band plays the complete melody for the first time at 2:33, like a story whose message is only revealed at the end.

The KC 4/4 had arrived, the tempo of the time: Page's walking bassline works as a rhythm pump while Basie's minimalist piano style moderates the dynamic call-and-response, grounding the constant dramatic interplay of soloists, sections, and rhythm. On tour a year later, "Moten Swing" thrilled the nation's most sophisticated dancers at Harlem's Savoy Ballroom with its buoyant groove.

Yet "Moten Swing" turned out to be the bandleader's swan song. Having hired Bill Basie on piano to focus on managing the band, he suffered a coup when the young pianist stole the band and renamed himself Count. Hailing from Red Bank, New Jersey, Basie learned piano watching Fats Waller play at the Lincoln Theater in Manhattan. He wound up stranded in Kansas City when his touring theatrical show ran out of funds. Basie figured out a new role for the swing piano: to moderate the call-and-response of soloist and section with short, well-timed solos. Basie's minimalist style of short blues riffs cut through big-band noise and allowed each section and the listener to reset for the next charge.

Everything came together for the Count Basie Orchestra during its three year residency at the Reno Club: Lester Young's melodic genius, Jo Jones' crisp drumming, Eddie Durham's arrangements. Walter Page's musical leadership on the bandstand. The Reno was a small club, just "a white place where ranchers would come in, all they served was beer and chili", Cliff Leeman recalled, but the first time he walked in, "I heard this band, and for a 15c beer, I almost fell on the floor". The club's live radio feed on Thursday nights could be heard all the way to Chicago and in 1936, two recording scouts rushed down to sign the band.

Columbia Records producer and talent scout John Hammond couldn't believe his ears when he entered the Reno Club: the Basie band was blowing the roof off the tiny dive with only nine musicians. "They weren't making much money and yet playing such powerful music", he recalled. Basie took Hammond around KC at dawn: first to the Sunset Club to hear Joe Turner, then to a jam session at the Cherry Blossom, and finally to a so-called "spook breakfast" of swing and soul food. When Hammond thought the night was finally over —at 11am— he found Lester Young sitting in with a blues guitarist, just jamming. Hammond brought the Count Basie Orchestra to New York, tightened its sound through personnel changes, then supervised its best recordings, such as Jimmy Rushing's joyful vocals on "Sent for You Yesterday" and "Between the Devil and the Deep Blue Sea".

In 1938, Hammond produced a famous two-day Carnegie Hall concert to show off the varieties of American music: "From Spirituals to Swing". The Basie Orchestra opened the program, played as a small unit (The Kansas City Six), and served as the house band for singers Jimmy Rushing and Helen Humes. Big Joe Turner and Pete Johnson sang their KC blues, Ida Cox represented for 1920s blueswomen, and Big Bill Broonzy brought his jazzy Chicago blues. Sister Rosetta Tharpe and the Golden Gate Quartet performed spirituals. Hammond had just signed jazz's first electric guitarist, Charlie Christian, and he played with Benny Goodman's band. The concert offered jazz as an artistic crucible that evolved from spirituals, blues, ragtime, New Orleans music, and Tin Pan Alley: big band jazz was now the national music.

Swinging Our Machines

KC's musical style confronted the artistic challenge of the Machine Age: how to integrate the machine rhythms of factories, traffic, and engines —the oppressive technological workplaces represented in films such as Metropolis and Modern Times— into society and culture. If New Orleans musicians first created enough human-powered noise to compete with machines, and Chicago musicians helped organize the joyful noise, KC's bands mastered the new industrial soundscape. The French modernist architect Le Corbusier made the connection when he visited the United States in 1936: "[T]he Negroes of the USA have breathed into jazz the song, the rhythm and the sound of machines".

Jazz Humanizes the Machine Age

The Kansas City style can be heard as an exciting, dynamic battle between teams of humans (big bands) and the urban, industrial environment (the technological soundscape). During the swing era (1930-1945), big bands grew in size to 15-18 musicians, streamlined their rhythm sections, and relied upon precise, unison section playing to create rhythmic momentum. The sections were akin to interlocking musical gears, driven by a flexible generator (the rhythm section), with constant interplay through short riffs. The new machine aesthetics of power, repetition, flow, volume, and precision were stylized and channeled into loud, propulsive songs for social dancing. These artists created a musical stylization of the Machine Age.

Here is the dialogue of jazz and industrialization in Count Basie's "Jumpin' at the Woodside". Basie's piano stomps off the time in a heavy, precise four-count. The sax section's first riff sounds an industrial hum —as of a power-line— that serves as both motif and foundation. Trumpets and trombones punctuate with overlapping staccato riffs until the band sounds like a factory's interlocking conveyor belts. A solo saxophone voice rises out of the mechanical rhythms and begins a call-and-response: the riff vibrates and sounds like bent notes on an electric guitar. A muted, vocalized trumpet solo follows, mocking and playful. Lester Young announces his solo with a deep honk —a train sound— then takes off at high speed while the rest of the sax section chase and challenge him.

A piano-led interlude follows, then the clarinet and a growling trumpet engage in call-and-response. Finally, the sax section returns to the opening riff at a higher pitch while the clarinet soars above it.

This technological dialogue was made possible by the Basie rhythm section, then known as "the All-American rhythm section" and still called "the greatest percussion combination in the history of jazz". Jo Jones lightened the band's power by keeping time on the shimmering high-hat, guitarist Freddie Green played precise quarter notes, Page propelled each soloist, and Basie's short riffs created exciting cross-rhythms.

Basie trombonist Dicky Wells described the band's rhythm section as akin to "a Cadillac with the force of a Mack truck". As one swing drummer recalled, "The Basie feeling was so different from the 4/4 thumping of other sections. Jo Jones's cymbals, the guitar and bass walking together, the plinking of Basie —it just lightened everything up. A revolutionary change had taken place".

The model for the industrial power of big bands was the rhythms and sounds of trains, or "locomotive onomatopoeia" in the evocative phrase of Albert Murray. Big bands generated enough power to stylize the momentum and drive of even an express train. It is no accident that two iconic swing-era songs focus on train rides, "Chattanooga Choo-Choo" and "Take the A Train"; Ellington even laid on the floor of his train car to absorb its rhythms. The train was also a key metaphor for freedom in African-American culture: the gospel train, the underground railroad, the Northbound train during the Great Migration.

Here are two examples. Andy Kirk and the Clouds of Joy's "9:20 Special" opens with the locomotive onomatopoeia of a train's arrival. The brass section strains at the start like the metal-on-metal of train brakes and the trumpet's sonorities resemble train whistles. The listener boards when the sax section shifts into the aural equivalent of a smooth ride, with the soloists making conversation against the train's clickety-clack rhythm. In the first minute, there is ten seconds of high brass track-clearing, a short piano riff, and then a luxurious groove over which muted trumpets argue with the saxophones (00:55). Mary Lou Williams slotted in some call-and-response with the brass before her piano solo. At the two-minute mark, the melody suddenly asserts itself as if blowing past local stations (@ 1:55). A gritty, soulful tenor solo returns us inside, honks like a train whistle, and we arrive at the next stop.

Harlan Leonard and his Rockets' "I Don't Want to Set the World on Fire" (1940) opens with ten seconds of locomotive onomatopoeia. Once up to speed, this big band train barely slows at all, forcing blues vocalist Myra Taylor out of her relaxed groove, as if chasing her to get up to speed (@ 1:35). In the last thirty seconds, the band creates the sensation of whirling circles of sound, as if the train might take off into the sky. This song was one of the band's "flagwavers" or "killer-dillers", slang for a band's fastest songs, the favorites of the best swing dancers.

The steam train was the most powerful and familiar machine in the *landscape* and this swing-era musical dialogue reflected a shared historical *soundscape*. Strange as it may sound, the train was the *muse* of the big-band era.

Arrangers, Riffs, and Unsung Jazz Lives

For two generations, the arranger was as important as the bandleader or star soloists. The arranger created each song's musical narrative through the deployment of *riffs*. A riff is a short repeated rhythmic phrase, typically used as an introduction or refrain in a song. Beethoven's Fifth opens with a riff —BA-BA-BA *BUH*, ba-ba-ba *buh*— as does the Rolling Stones' "Satisfaction" (da-da da-duh-*DA* de-DAH-da). In the KC style, riffs often became melodies with attributions for the original idea: "Lester Leaps In", "Dickie's Dream", "Mary's Idea". The creators of the riff-style were a distinctive trio of arrangers, each an unsung figure of multiple talents: trombonist Eddie Durham was a pioneer of the electric guitar; Mary Lou Williams was a major composer; Jesse Stone was an architect of rock-and-roll.

Riffs were the main content of the AABA song form —the main format of jazz standards— and sometimes known as the "American popular song form".

The AABA form emerged from Broadway show tunes in the early twentieth century and consists of four sections: an eight-bar A section; a second eight-bar A section, repeated with variation; a new eight-bar B section (different material), often called "the release" (or bridge); then a final eight-bar A section. In short, the riff is stated (A), repeated (A), set off by a new idea (B), then repeated a final time (A), often with variations.

"Lester Leaps In" is an accessible example since the riff is played *twice* in each A section: ba-da-*ba* ba ba-da-da *da*-da-da. Only Basie plays the release on piano (@ 00:18) and then the band repeats the riff. After the first pass of the AABA melody, Young takes off on his solo (@ 00:34). Listen to where he hits the "B" section (@ 00:49). Young and Basie then make it interesting: piano and tenor trade fours (four-bar ideas) during the A section and there is a stop-time chorus on the last section with the band punctuating on a riff.

In comparison, "Mary's Idea" is a much more sophisticated riff-style arrangement in the 32-bar AABA form. After only four bars (the initial statement of the "A" theme), Williams adds a counter-riff for the brass in the second half. The second time through has a separate variation but the theme is still clear. You can hear when the "B" section happens since only the saxophone section plays it, a beautiful "release". Then the band returns to the A theme and when it ends, the trumpet solo begins. The AABA form creates a memorable imprint without boring the listener. It also fits a common template in African-American culture more broadly: repetition with a difference, or a layer of disruption to create tension. In AABA, the "B" theme (the release) creates variety and disruption such that returning to the main riff is like coming home.

Jesse Stone claimed to have invented the riff style (and might have) but he conceded that its masters were Walter Page's Oklahoma City Blue Devils. Stone was raised middle-class in Kansas and Missouri: he was classically trained, heard spirituals from his aunts, and learned blues from his uncles. His grandfather organized the family into a successful minstrel show that traveled extensively in the Dakotas. In 1921, Stone heard the revolution of New Orleans jazz improvisation immediately: "I had never heard where everybody played for themselves [...] our things were patterned". Yet he felt its rhythm was too jerky and required a change in the "rhythm social order".

Stone formed a band that so impressed a local businessman he bought them uniforms and a bus then sent them north into Nebraska and the Dakotas. The band was so successful it traveled the region for nearly five years —until the musicians wanted to get back to "Black people and Black girls, their own people". Stone then brought his extensive musical knowledge to KC and always led or arranged one of its major bands: Jesse Stone's Blues Serenaders, the George E. Lee Orchestra, or the Thamon Hayes Band.

Eddie Durham was a well-traveled musician from San Marcos, Texas, and a key member of the Oklahoma City Blue Devils. "The Kansas City riff always carried a melody that you could write a song from. The riffs I heard up East, they didn't make good melodies". Durham and Basie were central to the band's success and he called the pianist "a master at creating and maintaining tempo". The two would write a theme together, sketch a quick arrangement, then take it out to the sections.

Each section then went off into a corner of the band room to generate underlying riffs —this was called a *head arrangement.* A trombonist might say, "how about if we play this —bah, bah-ra-RA-bah— while the sax section plays the main riff". And just like that, a theme became a song through practice, rehearsal, and refinement. "Band members collectively improvised in the studio around head arrangements memorized from sketched introductions", Harlan Leonard recalled. Musicians liked riffs that "allowed ample room for solo flights and interaction between sections", he said, qualities that "gave the city's music the kind of spontaneity in sound lacking in more polished, precise big band arrangements". With pride, Leonard added, "We made it up out of nothing".

Durham arranged many Basie classics, including the band theme, "One O'Clock Jump", as well as Glenn Miller's big hit, "In the Mood", and many others. Yet he is now better known as a pioneer of the electric guitar. To get the sound Durham heard in his mind, he first used a National guitar (with a built-in resonator) and plugged it right into a venue's sound system: "I'd just play solo work, and I was the only guy playing that kind of guitar in jazz". He played some of the earliest electric guitar solos on record (in 1938, with the Kansas City Six) but his impact was greater as the mentor of Charlie Christian, the instrument's pioneer in jazz.

Durham met the teen-aged guitarist in Oklahoma City while on tour with Basie. Christian had toured with Dallas's Alphonse Trent Band and wanted to play like him —"with class", he said. Durham showed him some quick, stylistic tricks: key rhythm patterns, quick riffs, playing the downstroke to get "a staccato sound and sound like a horn". Within a year, he was hired by Benny Goodman and played in the Spirituals to Swing concert. He then moved to New York and helped create bebop even as he was first mapping the sonic parameters of electric guitar in jazz.

Both Durham and Stone created and directed all-female bands in the 1940s: Eddie Durham's All-Star Girl Orchestra and Stone's International Sweethearts of Rhythm. Stone was the musical director of the Apollo Theater for two years then mentored altoist Louis Jordan, the major hitmaker and conduit between swing and rock-and-roll. Stone wrote "Shake, Rattle and Roll" and "Flip, Flop & Fly" for Joe Turner and he was a founding arranger and talent scout for Atlantic Records. In many ways, KC's riff-style arrangers carried forward the rhythmic and emotional content of the blues into bebop, rhythm-and-blues, and rock-and-roll.

A Solo Tells A Story: Lester Young, Billie Holiday, Ben Webster

A solo must *tell a story*, KC musicians said —in fact, it must tell *your* story. To "tell your story" meant both that you must have a story *to tell* —you must be "sayin' something"— and must have a distinctive artistic voice to tell it in. A musician chooses a model at first, but there comes a time to "show them that you're an individual", Lester Young said. "I played like [Frankie] Trumbauer when I was starting out. But then there's a time when you have to go out for yourself and *tell your story*". Like the writing style of an Ernest Hemingway, a Virginia Woolf, or a Gabriel Garcia Marquez, to be an individual means to create a personalized artistic sound and syntax. Young's sound revolutionized the tenor saxophone with its cool tone, long, flowing lines, and behind-the-beat rhythmic approach.

The solo evolved in KC due to its jam sessions since musicians treated these encounters like gunfights or duels out of frontier mythology. Drummer Lee Young once said of his brother (Lester), "anyone who picked up a saxophone, you know, Lester wanted some of it ... he really wanted to see who was the better man. It would be just like a prize fighter or a wrestler".

When trumpeter Buck Clayton moved to KC from California, word got out he would be at the Sunset Club. A few trumpeters came out to welcome and challenge him —they started jamming— but then, "half an hour later came three more trumpet players, [then] more and more trumpet players came in to blow", Clayton recalled. "To me, it seemed as if they were coming from all directions".

The Kansas City Six recording of "Lady Be Good" provides a good example of individual statement combined with group support and it was Young's first recorded solo. It starts with forty seconds of a piano trio featuring Basie's minimalist style, Page's heartbeat bass, and Jones' high-hat. Sonic platform established, Young's tenor saxophone steps in on the upbeat then ascends, working with the drummer's accents, then floats free of the beat while keeping the rhythm. Just when he seems finished with his 40-second solo, he lifts off into a new set of ideas for twenty seconds (@ 1:30). The trumpet then charges in and Young honks his support happily underneath him. The return of the piano trio provides some symmetry, then Young offers one last ten-second riff as if in joyous satisfaction of the band's performance.

Lester Young and Billie Holiday were musical soulmates. Holiday grew up in Baltimore and moved to New York in the 1930s but perfected her vocal approach during a one-year stint traveling with the Count Basie Orchestra. She began to think of herself as more of an improvisational jazz artist than a singer.

"I don't think I'm singing", she said, "I feel like I'm playing a horn. I try to improvise like Les Young, like Louis Armstrong".

Billie Holiday recorded nearly fifty classics between 1937-1942 in a genre of *chamber jazz* she practically invented, "a milestone in Western music", jazz critic Will Friedwald declaimed, on a continuum "from Bach to Mozart to Ornette Coleman". Unlike the pathos of her later work, Holiday's voice in this period balanced playful exuberance and affirmative emotional catharsis, as in the jaunty openings of "Me, Myself, and I" or "Laughing at Life". Holiday's voice was a singular mix of yearning, confession, resignation, affirmation, and survival. She turned jazz into a mode of individual, female resistance.

Two examples with Young show the range of Holiday's emotional spectrum. "He's Funny That Way" is a rapturous expression of adulation while "All of Me" is a pained, bittersweet confession of surrender to a cruel partner. In both standards, Holiday provides a controlled emotional flow of storytelling, from introductory mood to climactic moment.

Young's dreamy romantic intro leads into the first verse of "He's Funny That Way", a song about a self-reliant woman whose luck has suddenly turned: "never had nothing / no one to care", she complains then drops her voice slightly, as if in surprise, "[but] I've got a man / crazy for me". Young's sax works as a second voice behind Holiday's vocal, creating an unusual duet called an "obbligato", a simultaneous accompaniment. In effect, voice and tenor seem to act out the song's love. Young's sax dances around Holiday's vocal (1:05-1:22), leading into Buck Clayton's muted trumpet solo (1:23-1:53), a string of vocalized phrases that add up to a man expressing his love. In the third verse, vocal and saxophone entwine (2:00-2:30), leading to Holiday's climactic expression of joy, "I've got that man / *cra-zy* for me / He's funny that way!"

By way of contrast, the ambiguity of a love affair in "All of Me" starts with a relaxing mid-tempo piano intro that quiets to set up Holiday's sultry, ironic tale of a woman's loss of will. She first ticks off the parts of her body she no longer controls. The way Holiday infuses sorrow into certain words —"take my lips / I want to *loo-oose* them"— creates a shared experience with powerless lovers everywhere. Two verses in, Young's solo mirrors Holiday's romantic pathos: he floods the tone with a rich, bittersweet sound, an aural equivalent of binging on chocolate. In the third verse, Holiday's cry against the injustice of affection fights with the horn section's falling, descending riff. Young plays a quick, five-second warning call to stop her fall but fails. "You took the best", she sings, shorn of her powers, "so *why not* take the rest", she gives up, "Baby, take *all* of me". The pun is a paradox, as if she is falling upwards into an unfair, destructive relationship.

Joel
Dinerstein

QIJ - KC

Created by Joel Dinerstein · 13 songs, 39 min

PLAY (⋯)

FOLLOWERS
0

Download

Q Filter

#	TITLE	ARTIST	ALBUM		
♢	The Lady Who Swings the Band	Andy Kirk & His 12 Clou...	The Very Best Of	2019-05-25	2:49
♢	Moten Swing	Bennie Moten's Kansas...	Greatest Hits Series--S...	2019-05-30	3:24
♢	Sent For You Yesterday	Count Basie	The Complete Decca R...	2019-06-26	2:59
♢	Jumpin' At The Woodside	Count Basie	The Complete Decca R...	2019-06-11	3:10
♢	9:20 Special	Andy Kirk	Great Jazz Bands	2019-05-25	3:26
♢	Mary's Idea	Mary Lou Williams	Queen of Jazz Piano	2020-04-22	3:04
♢	Oh, Lady Be Good! (78rpm Version)	Jones-Smith, Incorpora...	The Columbia, Okeh &...	2019-06-10	3:08
♢	He's Funny That Way - Take 1	Billie Holiday	A Musical Romance	2020-04-22	2:38
♢	All of Me (with Eddie Heywood & His Orchestra)	Billie Holiday, Eddie He...	Lady Day: The Complet...	2020-04-22	3:01
♢	Cotton Tail	Duke Ellington	Never No Lament: The ...	2020-04-22	3:11
♢	Swingmatism	Jay McShann & His Or...	The Essential Collection	2019-06-03	2:50
♢	Shake, Rattle and Roll	Big Joe Turner	Shake, Rattle and Roll	2020-04-22	3:00

4. Dinerstein's Kansas City playlist.

By accenting only certain words or notes through rhythmic nuance and the manipulation of musical space, Holiday's chamber jazz created a low-key late-night emotional sphere of adult experience. In these tunes, Holiday's voice and Young's saxophone curl around each other, shape the air into sound, rise into smoky swirls of late-night yearning, then settle into your clothes with the bittersweet taste of romance come and gone.

Holiday's creation of a sound and style from personal experience made her *the* model for singers from Frank Sinatra, Anita O'Day, and Dinah Washington to Cassandra Wilson to Amy Winehouse. To pianist Teddy Wilson, the director of Holiday's chamber jazz sessions, "her singing, in a very integral way, was a reflection of her whole psychology, her experience". Together with Young, Holiday transformed the blues into an urbane American romanticism, a *cool aesthetic* re-tooled by Sinatra and others into a global musical style.

Ben Webster's tenor sound is one of jazz's most vocalized styles, by turn either breathy, whispering, and romantic or growling, clawing, and protesting. A KC native, Webster sat in the sax sections of Bennie Moten's and Andy Kirk's bands as an acolyte of Hawkins's tenor sound. Webster's art projects an inner desire for beauty that seems contrary to his personality as a brawling, hard-drinking man. Yet he was the first tenor saxophonist ever hired by Duke Ellington and one of his early solos with the band models jazz's artistic ideal of improvising soloist and ensemble response.

"Cotton Tail" opens with a springy, swinging bass supporting the sax section's lustrous sound and the energy quickly escalates through a call-and-response between the raucous trombone and the surging saxes. Webster enters softly with a set of short, melodic phrases and soon the brass sections shout back with staccato pulse bursts. Just after he holds and twirls a single note, he escalates up the scale to the song's first climax (1:10) with the band falling in with joyful accord. After Ellington's ten-second interlude, we are suddenly immersed in an elegant, harmonious musical bridge played by five saxophones! It almost sounds like a different song until the trumpets charge back in, take over for twenty seconds, and then the sax section re-states the melody one last time.

Webster became the most admired balladeer of standards in jazz history after his three years with the Duke ("My Funny Valentine", "Cry Me A River", "Pennies From Heaven"). Known affectionally as "The Brute", Webster's whispered tone and thoughtful melodic treatments suggest a new form of singing. A favorite of European audiences, Webster spent his final decade living and playing in Copenhagen, where the city named a street for him, "Ben Websters Vej".

But it was Charlie Parker who transformed the solo into the central artistic feature of jazz. While in high school, Parker haunted KC's jam sessions, taking Lester Young as his first idol and learning his solos note-for-note. He then shifted his model to altoist Buster Smith but double-timed Smith's liquid linear flow, leaving musicians slack-jawed at his speed and precision. As the star soloist of KC's last great swing band —the Jay McShann Orchestra— Parker's solo on the hit "Swingmatism" shows off his early, flint-edged soaring blues sound (1:52-2:16).

The Lost Jazz City Moves to New York

In effect, the Kansas City music workshop packed up and took its principles to New York, the center of the jazz world. Its jam session culture moved to Harlem nightclubs such as Minton's and Monroe's, where Parker, Young, Webster, Christian, and Mary Lou Williams often played deep into the night. Williams ran a musical salon out of her Harlem apartment and taught music theory to a generation. She also became a composer in New York, recording her masterpiece, *Zodiac Suite* (1945), combining jazz, classical, and boogie-woogie elements. Other KC musicians moved to Los Angeles and sparked its Central Avenue scene.

Unlike Chicago and New Orleans, the Kansas City scene only lasted twenty years or so. Akin to Chicago, when reform forces shut down the Pendergast political machine, the money and musicians moved to both coasts. Director Robert Altman tried and failed to capture the aural luminescence of this scene in *Kansas City* (1997), but the soundtrack contains two

Count Basie songs which an all-star jazz unit catches the city's communal musical culture. An upbeat elegy for the city survives in "Goin' to Kansas City" (1952), a rhythm-&-blues hit written as a tribute to Big Joe Turner by the Jewish songwriting team of Jerry Leiber and Mike Stoller.

Big Joe Turner was a pioneer of rock-and-roll through his foundational hits of "Shake, Rattle, & Roll" and "Flip, Flop & Fly" —both written by Jesse Stone. Yet Turner always said he had been singing the same way since 1925 and rock-and-roll "wasn't but a different name for the same music I've been singing all my life". Jazz, blues, swing, rhythm-and-blues, rock-and-roll —these were just genre names. In 1952, Turner made a classic jazzy blues album that *did* capture the Kansas City spirit —*Boss of the Blues*— backed by members of Basie's and Ellington's bands. In the early 1960s, the Count Basie Orchestra made three excellent albums with Frank Sinatra, a swan song for the human-powered big bands.

In 1939, Coleman Hawkins recorded "Body & Soul", a six-chorus saxophone concerto and surprise hit. Jazz musicians often said about it, "He did all you could do with a song", and this, too, signaled that jazz had hit a plateau. Hawkins and Lester Young were in another jam session that year in New York. They traded choruses for a while and suddenly Hawkins walked off the stage, confident in his victory. But Young got the last laugh: he followed Hawkins, hooting him off-stage and out the door with saxophone honks, refusing to concede. Their styles were the poles of tenor saxophone for a generation —Hawkins working vertically through the chords, Young with his flowing, horizontal lines— until John Coltrane and Sonny Rollins created new directions on the instrument.

When drummer Cliff Leeman used to run into Jo Jones in New York, they would just roll their eyes and shake their heads, "Whew —Kansas City", one would say, "no one would even believe it". Charlie Parker's mentor, Buster Smith, once left a more telling epitaph in an interview: "All of them cats. Ben Webster, Herschel Evans, Lester Young —always quiet, sitting over in the corner. All them tenor saxes. All of them artists".

Chapter 4

New York: The Golden Age of Jazz, 1945-1965

Duke Ellington's "Take the A Train" (1941) originated as written subway directions for his young arranger, Billy Strayhorn, to get to his Harlem apartment. New York was home to the Cotton Club, the Charleston, the Savoy Ballroom, and Gershwin's "Rhapsody in Blue" in the 1920s, yet it had no signature jazz *style*. It did have Ellington —the elegant, urbane composer whose compositions burst open with new tonal colors, innovative structures, and imaginative soloists. "Take the A Train" became the Duke's signature song: it polished the propulsive swing of Kansas City with a touch of elegance, streamlining the industrial cacophony of a subway ride into smooth, seared industrial horn-lines. And it marks the orchestra's peak years as its two new hires —KC's Ben Webster and bassist Jimmy Blanton— brought the hard-swinging sound of the territory bands to New York.

Just across Harlem, Dizzy Gillespie and KC's Charlie "Bird" Parker were instigating a paradigm shift in jazz from big band swing to small units of soloists. Two clubs were jazz workshops —Minton's and Monroe's— where Parker's speed and phrasing, pianist Thelonious Monk's melodic imagination, and Kenny Clarke's creative beats changed the very conception of jazz as an art form. Altoists who had aspired to lyricism were now mesmerized by Bird's quicksilver harmonic changes; Gillespie's lightning-fast high-register trumpet runs made Armstrong's measured phrasing seem obsolete. Soldiers returning home from World War II barely recognized jazz, as any quick comparison of "Take the 'A' Train" and Parker's "Koko" will show.

When bebop moved downtown to "swing street" (West 52nd Street), it quickly became the epicenter of the jazz world. Musicians from every era could be found playing on "the Street": New Orleans legends, big bands, Chicago jazz at Condon's, R&B combos, Billie Holiday's cabaret swing. Arranger Gil Evans met four of his jazz heroes his first night on the Street, including Webster and Lester Young. Along this strip of hip clubs, jazz became the symbol of a new anti-racist stance among young musicians: as Gillespie later reflected, "52nd Street was the only non-prejudiced street in America".

Joel
Dinerstein

QJD - NYC

Created by Joel Dinerstein · 30 songs, 4 hr 13 min

FOLLOWERS
0

PLAY

Download

#	TITLE	ARTIST	ALBUM		
♢	Take the "A" Train	Duke Ellington	Never No Lament: The …	2019-10-18	2:55
♢	Koko - Original Take 2	Charlie Parker	The Charlie Parker Story	2019-10-22	2:54
♢	Carolina Shout	James P. Johnson	Father Of The Stride Pi…	2019-10-24	2:43
♢	Tea For Two	Art Tatum	I Got Rhythm Vol. 3 193…	2019-10-26	2:36
♢	A Little Max (Parfait) - Remastered	Duke Ellington	Money Jungle	2020-04-23	2:59
♢	It Don't Mean A Thing (If It Ain't Got That Swing)	Thelonious Monk	Plays Duke Ellington (K…	2020-04-23	4:42
♢	Ornithology	Charlie Parker	The Complete Savoy &…	2020-04-23	3:02
♢	Night In Tunisia	Dizzy Gillespie	Night In Tunisia: The Ve…	2019-10-24	3:08
♢	Brilliant Corners	Thelonious Monk, Sonn.	Brilliant Corners	2019-10-24	7:44
♢	Moanin'	Art Blakey	Moanin' (The Rudy Van…	2020-04-23	9:31
♢	I Could Write A Book	Miles Davis Quintet	Relaxin' With The Miles	2019-11-03	5:08
♢	Concierto de Aranjuez: Adagio	Miles Davis	Sketches of Spain	2020-04-23	16:22

5. Dinerstein's New York City playlist, 1.

Bebop created the standard format of jazz: small-unit conversation with a structure of *theme—solos—theme*. Bebop also codified jazz's core artistic challenges: to create a signature sound, manage split-second improvisational response, and make a personal statement in a solo. Since many young musicians lacked the musical theory for bebop, three teachers held after-hours tutorials: Gil Evans at his basement crashpad (aka "the 52nd Street annex"); Mary Lou Williams at her Harlem apartment; and Gillespie everywhere, since musicians followed him around. Out of these music salons came cool jazz (from Evans), Latin jazz (Gillespie), the West Coast jazz style, and other musical experiments.

This golden age of jazz peaked in 1959 with the release of seven masterpieces: *Kind of Blue* (Miles Davis), *Mingus Ah Um* (Charles Mingus), *Giant Steps* (John Coltrane), *Portrait in Jazz (Bill Evans), Time Out* (Dave Brubeck), *Alone in San Francisco* (Thelonious Monk), *The Shape of Jazz To Come* (Ornette Coleman). Jazz moved again, this time to Greenwich Village clubs such as the Five Spot, Half Note, and Village Vanguard. These clubs were incubators for the piano trios of Bill Evans, the workshops of Charles Mingus, and Ornette Coleman's free jazz units. Jazz improvisation influenced Village bohemia across art forms: Beat Generation writers, abstract expressionist painters, and rebel comedians such as Lenny Bruce, all transposed jazz method into their art forms.

Artistic freedom was always part of jazz's DNA and it was the political fuel for this golden age, which ran concurrent with the civil rights movement. The melding of artistic genius and ethnic soundings became explicit in Sonny Rollins' *Freedom Suite* (1958), Max Roach's *We Insist: Freedom Now Suite* (1960), Charles Mingus' "Fables of Faubus", and Art Blakey's *The Freedom Rider* (1964). *Where else but in jazz was there freedom for African-Americans?* Miles Davis was one of the world's most well-known jazz musician in 1959 yet he was arrested under a nightclub marquee with his own name on it. To the NYPD, he was just a black man transgressing on white supremacy by helping a white woman into a car.

In the 1960s, jazz exploded into multiple lines of exploration. Gillespie, Coltrane, and drummer Max Roach brought in rhythms and timbres from Africa, India, and Cuba. Ornette Coleman created "free jazz" and led musicians to break away from chords and scales. Pharoah Sanders and Alice Coltrane layered meditation, Eastern religion, and Buddhist chanting onto African percussion. Miles Davis brought rock, funk, and electric instruments into jazz, spurring musicians in his orbit to create fusion, the dominant jazz genre of the 1970s.

In the 1980s, New Orleans trumpeter Wynton Marsalis established Jazz at Lincoln Center —the music's first institutional home— and codified a jazz tradition. Yet the city's downtown jazz scene was also in a roiling state of experimentation. Musicians mixed punk, funk, industrial noise, and classical music into free jazz through new ensembles: John Zorn's Naked City, the World Saxophone Quartet, Henry Threadgill's Air. Jazz is a global music and New York remains the music's headquarters, where young musicians experiment and find fellow artists to take their playing to the next level.

Before Bebop

Fats Waller, James P. Johnson, and Willie "The Lion" Smith were an unholy trinity of New York pianist-composers whose *stride piano* shaped the tempo of 1920s nightlife. Johnson composed "The Charleston" (the dance) and a virtuosic test-piece for jazz pianists, "Carolina Shout". Fats Waller's comic virtuosity infiltrated New York theater with hit songs such as "Ain't Misbehavin'", "Honeysuckle Rose", "This Joint is Jumpin'", and "(What Did I Do To Be So) Black and Blue". The Lion called *stride piano* "Eastern ragtime", referring to the strong left (bass) hands of East Coast pianists who inflected more percussive drive into its melodies; they also improvised with tricks, lush embellishments, and novelty figures. The trio helped transform Tin Pan Alley melodies into jazz standards and The Lion struck an early iconic jazz pose: the raconteur at the piano with derby and cigar, smoke swirling around his mystery and mastery. Ellington apprenticed to The Lion's stride style and a young

George Gershwin absorbed jazz sitting under Smith's piano at Harlem rent parties.

Then one night, during a 1933 cutting contest of standards, a blind pianist from Ohio walked into a Harlem club and stole the piano crown. With startling virtuosity, Art Tatum played orchestral renditions of "Tea for Two" and "Tiger Rag", taking the latter at the amazing speed of *350bpm* and integrating octave jumps with cascading runs. Influenced by Waller and Earl Hines, Tatum's speed of thought, rollercoaster runs, and harmonic invention remain unmatched. Tatum and Waller quickly became close friends and drinking buddies —yet even so, whenever Tatum walked into a club, Waller closed the piano and said, "Ladies and gentlemen, *God* is in the house".

Tatum's first solo piano job in New York was at the Onyx Club on *52nd Street*, yet his solo genius did not fit well with bebop. Count Basie once said of Tatum, "He didn't like leaving any spaces", and it helps explain his lack of heirs as his busy virtuosity left little room for jazz conversation. Tatum's only major heir was Oscar Peterson, unlike Parker, whose musical breakthroughs transformed the approach to every instrument. Yet just before his death in 1956, Tatum found a perfect melodic foil in Ben Webster for an album of standards in which the saxophonist's spare, bluesy poetics blow smoke over Tatum's virtuosic imagination (*The Tatum Group Masterpieces, Vol. 8*).

The counterpart to stride piano was Fletcher Henderson's Orchestra. A college graduate with degrees in chemistry and math, Henderson could not find work in these fields due to racism. The pianist and bandleader codified the big band machine's sections into brass, reeds, and rhythm, with the help of his arranger, Don Redman. Henderson held down a residency at the Roseland Ballroom for twenty years, with a band featuring star soloist Coleman Hawkins and his band book was the foundation of Benny Goodman's success.

Duke Ellington came up as a stride pianist yet considered *the orchestra* his real instrument: his music was a synthesis of stride, big band power, and the classical harmonies of Debussy and Ravel. Ellington's singular *oeuvre* runs the gamut from three-minute pop masterpieces to concertos for individual bandmembers, from swing dance numbers ("It Don't Mean A Thing If It Ain't Got That Swing") to jazz standards ("Satin Doll"), from sacred concerts to folk-based suites from the orchestra's travels (*Far East Suite, Latin American Suite)*. When Ellington left space on the music score for his soloists to improvise ("ad lib here"), he empowered jazz as a democratic musical form; his thematic works about African-American life (*Black, Brown & Beige, A Drum is a Woman*) were akin to artistic treatises demanding equality for his people.

Two classic jazz albums illuminate how stride piano remained integral to Ellington's work and New York jazz. *Money Jungle* is a trio record wherein Ellington enters into battle with bassist Charles Mingus and bebop drummer Max Roach and they create thrilling trio interplay. On the title track, Ellington plays with a rare verve —vigorous left-hand rhythmic drive and dashed-off trills— yet inflected through bebop's focus on each chord's internal workings. "A Little Max (Parfait)" is Ellington's tonal portrait of the drummer and Roach deftly moves around the trap-set as if dancing on the drums. The lilting, minor-key "Fleurette Africaine" ("African Flower") features Mingus' feathery bassline, a sound like light rain that irrigates the piano's slow cascades and Roach's muted tom-toms.

Stride meets bebop in *Thelonious Monk Plays Duke Ellington* (1955). Monk grew up in New York and here marks his artistic debt to Duke through a set of musical implosions. He strips Ellington's classics to their bones, releasing the underlying beauty of each melody. For each, he deconstructs stride piano's fluid runs and decorative flourishes into plucked, resonant, accented rhythmic phrases, as on "It Don't Mean a Thing". At times, he twirls melodic motifs around two fingers like arabesques —yet even then, he defers the song's tempo until ready to move onto the next section, as on "I Let A Song Go Out of My Heart". You can practically hear Monk think through each improvisatory choice at his slow, cooled pace.

Where once a stride pianist used the song as a structure for improvisation, embellishment, and entertainment, now every musician infused their sound and style into each composition. With bebop, the creative soloist displaced the arranger, songwriter, and the song itself, upending the hierarchy of jazz values. Jazz had become conversation.

"Scrapple From the Apple": Bird, Diz, and Bebop

The bebop generation of African-American musicians was an artistic cohort as essential to global music as the French Impressionists were to art. The bebop generation rejected jazz's relationship to dance and pop music, redirecting it to individual development and innovation. In bebop's streaked solo runs, fast, angular rhythms, and complex harmonies, we can hear the first soundings of political protest: Charlie Parker's "Now's The Time" (1945) validated a Black vernacular street phrase that meant, *now's the time to protest*; Martin Luther King, Jr. invoked the phrase as a trope in his "I Have A Dream" speech a generation later. "Bebop was my generation's hiphop", novelist Ishmael Reed reflected, "we [even] dressed like beboppers", meaning the bérets, shades, and goatees favored by Gillespie and Monk.

Bebop's Rebel Music Theorists

Jazz musicians became rebel music theorists seeking new approaches. They studied classical, African, and non-Western musics, attuning themselves to an internal rhythmic sense akin to an "inner metronome". After bebop, jazz required an apprenticeship within a set of foundational Black musical practices —improvisation, swing, call-and-response, blue notes, vocalized timbre, gospel chords— that now constituted the *sound-world* of the form.

Bebop was art music, not pop or dance music: swing-era audiences often heard it as harsh, abrasive, and unmelodic. Even many swing-era musicians rejected bebop —including Lester Young and Louis Armstrong, who called it "Chinese music".

What was bebop, musically? Bird was listening to "Cherokee" one day and wondered what would happen if he soloed only on the highest notes of the chords such as the sevenths or ninths (the "tips", he called them) or even the elevenths and thirteenths? He experimented and then shared the method with Gillespie. Since Bird was a rebel, loner, and heroin addict, Gillespie taught Parker's breakthrough to other musicians. "Dizzy is a saint", drummer Kenny Clarke reflected, "[he] taught all the trumpet players and the drummers, too. He gave more of himself than any musician I know of —much more than Bird, because Bird was like a prophet who brings a message and disappears". Bebop was a paradigm shift in jazz carried off through the models and mentorship of "Bird and Diz".

Bebop reflected technological change and the aesthetic challenge of velocity: musical thinking at a breakneck New York pace reflected the atomic age. The unison burst of speed Bird and Diz breathe together to open "KoKo" shows their shared revolution: Parker's solo break into the stratosphere still defies belief (1:05-2:05) —to play that fast and clean with a blues edge— and he does it again on "Ornithology" (00:42-1:22). Gillespie recalled how Parker would be "at a tempo way up there and he'd 'cram' something in at triple the tempo that he was already playing", or as Miles Davis summed it up, "that whole [bebop] movement was conducive to [the] acceleration of everything". To borrow a Parker song title, bebop was a "Scrapple From the Apple".

To create a signature sound was especially liberating for bassists and drummers, since they had mostly kept time for dancers. Kenny Clarke's style was called "dropping bombs", a wartime reference to how he forced soloists to respond to disruptive accents. "Kenny's style of drumming, with 'bombs' in the bass drum and regular rhythm in the cymbals", Gillespie recalled, "infused a new conception into the dialogue of the drum that is now *the* dialogue". In addition, the bass became a solo instrument in the hands of Charles Mingus, Paul Chambers, and Oscar Pettiford.

Gillespie's development came more through cross-cultural exploration: he invented Latin jazz. When the first wave of Cuban and Puerto Rican musicians came to New York in the 1930s, he became friends with Mario Bauza, a former trumpeter with the Havana Symphony then with Cab Calloway's big band. Gillespie learned the clave beat and complex Cuban rhythms while becoming a good rumba dancer. In 1941, Bauza became musical director of Machito and his Afro-Cubans —hard-swinging big band known as "Count Basie with a clave beat"— and Gillespie often sat in. His first hit, "Manteca" (1947), mixed conga-driven grooves with bebop solos.

Gillespie then hired Chano Pozo, a master drummer from an Afro-Cuban "abakwa", a secret religious society tracing its rhythms back to the Yoruba people of West Africa. Pozo taught Gillespie's big band how to play polyrhythms by giving each bandmember a drum and a specific rhythm. Soon Pozo had everyone playing with and against different rhythms on the tour bus. The result was the two-part Cubop suite, "Cubana Be/Cubana Bop", a centerpiece of the band's concerts for a generation.

Gillespie's most well-known composition, "Night in Tunisia", grafts a North African theme onto an Afro-Cuban bassline. This now-global standard was a showcase for Dizzy's skillset: a catchy melody, an irresistible groove, call-and-response, fiery trumpet calls —all within a jazz-pop structure. The band slowly builds a groove then a quick shift to a counter-riff sets up Dizzy's entrance, a piercing line that lifts off into the upper register. Gillespie enfolds the melody into his solo then descends to hand the song off to Don Byas' sax solo.

Thelonious Monk played the piano like a drum —he struck the keys with flat fingers, accented each note to an off-kilter beat, and favored unusual consecutive intervals (like seconds and sixths in "Misterioso"). Monk's percussive approach changed how the instrument could be heard (and played) through an innovative stylistic array of accents, fragments, and dissonances. His sound was so original and alien, it took jazz musicians a decade to hear its strange beauty, despite compelling melodies such as "Ruby, My Dear", "Crepuscule With Nellie", and "Let's Cool One". The iconic "'Round Midnight" hauntingly evokes the soundscape of a person walking in solitude along slick urban streets.

Brilliant Corners (1957) captures Monk's originality as a composer. The title track's startling, back-breaking tempo changes alternately downshift and double-time. The listener gets caught up in its maze-like rhythmic shifts yet we are carried along by punctuating horn riffs, Rollins' soulful tenor solo, and the rolling dynamics of piano, drum, and sax. The composition reflects the rapid, uneven changes of the Cold War and the challenge of creating innovation from paradox —after all, *how can corners be brilliant*? Sonny Rollins referred to Monk as his "guru", as did John Coltrane. Other Monk-Rollins collaborations make swinging joyful jewels of jazz standards ("I Want To Be Happy") while the Monk-Coltrane quartet investigated compositions in a more mathematical way.

Sonny Rollins Under the Williamsburg Bridge

Rollins can also lay claim to the most impressive example of self- and musical development in the era: he withdrew from the scene for two years and instead played every night on the Williamsburg Bridge. Rollins had hit a musical plateau and he was sick of the racism in the jazz business. Rather than disturb his neighbors with late-night practicing, Rollins found the nearby bridge to be "a private place I can blow my horn as loud as I want". He built a stronger, more controlled sound by playing into the industrial mix of car, subway, and harbor traffic, a musician in dialogue with the city's soundscape. This experience is commemorated in *The Bridge* (1962), one of his finest albums.

A young journalist named George W. Goodman lived in Rollins' building at the time and thought of him simply as "Mr. Cool" for his rebellion, sound, and determination. Our modern concept of cool was created by Lester Young and his heirs, Bird and Miles Davis: cool meant a mix of calmness, relaxed style, and stoic defiance, yet also originality and integrity. Bebop compositions mark the concept's original meanings of relaxation and emotional self-control in the face of racism: Parker's "Cool Blues", Monk's "Let's Cool One", Lester Young's "Just Coolin'", Sonny

Clark's "Cool Struttin'", Howard McGhee's "Cool". Goodman left us his useful concise definition: "Cool was defiance with dignity".

Miles Davis once remarked that bebop was too fast for most listeners to hear its speed, phrasing, humor, and virtuosity. The solution was *hard bop* and this New York style remains a common jazz format. So what is the difference?

Hard bop reintegrated jazz with groove-driven forms such as blues, gospel, soul, and R&B: its compositions have simple, memorable themes played by a frontline of horns. Hard bop ensembles feature six or seven pieces such that its themes blast out like heraldic calls while the successive, passionate solos create exciting live performances. Hard bop was also often more ethnically conscious, as these jazz hits of the 1950s suggest: Horace Silver's "The Preacher", Lee Morgan's "The Sidewinder", Max Roach and Clifford Brown's "Blues Walk", Cannonball Adderley's "Mercy, Mercy, Mercy".

Art Blakey and the Jazz Messengers were the archetypal group of hard bop: the drummer led a band akin to a doctoral program and mentored two generations of musicians, from Wayne Shorter to Wynton Marsalis. *Moanin'* is a classic hard bop album and its title track has a bluesy theme, gospel chords, and four distinctively developed solos. The bluesy theme proceeds for a full minute through the piano's call-and-response with the horns until Blakey's drum roll explodes through the intro and makes room for the trumpet's fiery two-minute solo. Wayne Shorter makes a chill entrance on tenor then climbs passionately up the scale; the piano recalls the theme then builds in intensity; a bass solo clears our heads and leads back to the theme. Respect and support established for each musician, the band spends the last minute in satisfying, collective grooving.

In "Moanin", each solo has its own narrative with a beginning, middle and end. The trumpet starts out fiery then measures and mellows out; the saxophone starts out with short, relaxed phrases then becomes exploratory, angry, and soulful, spiking up to a climax; the piano rolls out a few blues chords then works up to dramatic runs in his right hand and pounding chords with his left. The listening experience is *cumulative*: this is a conversation and each solo is a person speaking.

Blakey's cultural politics and ethnic pride were always in play. He dedicated *The Freedom Rider* (1961) to those civil rights workers risking their lives to end Jim Crow segregation. He then recorded *The African Beat* (1962) with a mix of African and jazz musicians who had traveled to Africa. Playing mostly Nigerian music, the ensemble featured talking drums, bata drums, congas, timpani, log drums, and telegraph drums, along with percussion such as gongs and maracas, *shekere* and *mbira*. Throughout the 1970s, the Messengers opened every gig with "Lift Every Voice and Sing", a song sometimes called "the Black national anthem".

Charlie Parker died in 1954 at thirty-four, so exhausted by his life of excess, artistic achievement, and heroin addiction that the doctor thought him a man of fifty-four. Mingus composed two elegies, "Bird Calls" and "Gunslinging Bird". Parker's addiction played a pernicious role in his hero-worship: musicians thought the drug assisted his genius even as he hated hearing musicians tried heroin in his name. Pianist Hampton Hawes explained the reasons why his friend and mentor chose heroin:

He hated the black-white split and what was happening to his people, couldn't come up with an answer so he stayed high. Played, fuck, drank, and got high. The way he lived his life was telling everyone[:] You don't dig me, you don't dig my people, you don't dig my music... [He] didn't answer to nobody but himself 'cause [then] when you go, you go down alone.

Saxophonist Don Byas was once asked if bebop had been a form of social protest: "I'm always trying to make my sound stronger and more brutal than ever. I shake the walls in the joints I play in. *I'm always trying to sound brutal without losing the beauty*, in order to impress people and wake them up", he said. "My form of protest is to play as hard and strong as

I am". Bebop allowed for the affirmation of freedom through the sheer artistic power of one individual against the world.

Miles Davis: Cool, Lyrical, Modal, Funk, Fusion

> *"Listen. The greatest feeling I ever had in my life —with my clothes on— was when I first heard Diz and Bird together in St. Louis in 1944. I was 18 years old… It was a motherfucker. The way that band was playing music —that was* all *I wanted to hear".*

These are the opening lines of *Miles: The Autobiography* and this encounter constitutes a remarkable artistic convergence. Miles came to New York and joined Parker's band at the age of eighteen but a decade later, as Davis went, so went the future of jazz —not least since John Coltrane, Cannonball Adderley, Herbie Hancock, Wayne Shorter, Jack DeJohnette, Chick Corea, and John McLaughlin emerged from his bands. You can hear the jazz eras change just through his trumpet *sound*: it shifts from muted lyrical beauty (1950s) to fiery open-bell declarations (1960s) to short, staccato blasts with electronic effects (1970s).

Miles Davis was jazz's Picasso —a restless artist with several creative periods, an aural painter of soundscapes, the first crossover Black icon of cool. Davis' gruff voice, his open-ended leadership style, his strategic silences in music *and* life —all informed a fierce mask meant to keep white people at a distance. "Miles Davis was a very shy guy who created a kind of hostile persona to keep people away from him", his friend Quincy Jones said, "Miles was not going to be Louis Armstrong". Davis turned his back on audiences when soloing and refused the role of entertainer; in his private life, he drove a Ferrari around Manhattan and was chosen one of America's best-dressed men.

Miles Davis moved to New York to be on the cutting-edge of jazz and quit Julliard to hang out on *The Street* —bebop's innovations felt more urgent than his music theory classes. Parker hired Davis as a lyrical foil to his alto virtuosity, an apprenticeship that left Davis with a heroin habit. When Davis quit cold-turkey in 1954, he became a bandleader and began two decades of nonstop creative production.

Bebop was never Davis' métier —his musical strengths were lyricism, succinct phrasing, a melodic sense of timing. Like Billie Holiday, he chose the "important notes" through sculpted short phrases that told a non-verbal story. Miles favored the middle range over the high, piercing runs preferred by Armstrong and Gillespie. This led to his innovation of "flooding the tone": Davis put the trumpet's bell right up against the microphone such that his barest whisper became amplified. In effect, Davis utilized electricity as an artistic device to transform the sound of his acoustic instrument.

The vocalized phrasing, the muted trumpet, staying in the middle range —this trio of choices created a trumpet sound akin to the human male voice. "People tell me my sound is like a human voice", Davis said, "and that's what I want it to be". In fact, his sound was influenced by *specific* voices: "I learned a lot about phrasing listening to the way Frank Sinatra, Nat Cole, and even Orson Welles phrased", he wrote, praising each for "the way they shape a musical line or sentence or phrase with their voice".

Take "If I Were A Bell" or "It Never Entered My Mind", Broadway showtunes that Miles transformed into meditative jazz standards. Davis' solos are characterized by dramatic entrances, short melodic phrases, impeccable timing, slow fades, and creative silence. And *flooding the tone* makes Davis' sound liqueous: each note seems to enter the listener's mind and crystallize, leaving a musical watermark.

Davis developed his timing through several collaborations with arranger Gil Evans. The relationship began with the *Birth of the Cool* recordings (1949-50), a nine-piece inter-racial group combining jazz and classical music: these were more linear compositions, with arrangements and short solos. This was *cool jazz*, a countermove to bebop that featured orchestrations, strings, and *cooler* (softer) instrumental tones.

In the 1950s, Miles and Evans shared an affinity for well-defined melodies, complex musical textures, and the call-and-response of solo-and-orchestra, as illuminated in the classic *Sketches of Spain* (1960). On the opening track, "Concierto de Aranjuez", a slow, quiet rhythm played on maracas baits our ears for a sudden orchestral blast of beautiful colors, as if someone switched on a bank of lights in your mind. Evans shifts the background a little and Miles enters to play the melody: his trumpet floats up, into, and through the massed strings and horns. With its flamenco themes and imaginative arrangements, the album expanded the possibilities of jazz.

The Miles Davis Quintet was then also revolutionizing jazz through the modal music of *Kind of Blue*. Modal jazz opened up new possibilities for soloing that led to more of a horizontal flow based on modes rather than bebop's major and minor chordal explorations. "So What", the opening track, depends upon the bebop format —theme, three solos, theme— yet its effect is also cumulative and textural, as in cool jazz. Pianist Bill Evans and bassist Paul Chambers set a quasi-classical mood for thirty seconds, then the bass plays the distinctive nine-note theme. The three solos reveal jazz's core artistic gift to the arts, the personalized instrumental sound. Davis improvises on (and around) the melody with resonant short phrases. Coltrane's solo then pursues the scales and their inversions with intensity, heat, and upward leaps. Cannonball Adderley echoes

Coltrane's phrasing at first then breaks free to bounce down a few chords to find a motif. The band then vamps with intermittent horn riffs pressing upon the piano solo. By the eight-minute mark, it is as if our reality has been subsumed by this sound-world created in the studio.

Each member of this quintet became a bandleader with an influential vision. Bill Evans created the blueprint for piano trio interplay; Adderley led a hard-swinging sextet, the standard-bearer of soul jazz. John Coltrane explored African polyrhythms, musical theory, free jazz, and spiritual communion. Paul Chambers and Jimmy Cobb became known as *the* rhythm section and each appeared on many classic albums. Their musical visions were made possible by Davis's egalitarian leadership model: musicians showed up to a session ready-to-play without direction and were expected to add their innovations to the skeletal outlines of songs.

By 1964, Miles Davis' second great quintet was in place (1965-1969), featuring bassist Ron Carter, the young drummer Tony Williams, and two graduates of Blakey's Messengers, pianist Herbie Hancock and saxophonist Wayne Shorter. This quintet often played faster and more freely with solos that sizzled as if off the grill before melting back into melodies (*Live at the Plugged Nickel*). Hancock and Shorter developed into major composers: Hancock wrote the standards "Watermelon Man" and "Cantaloupe Island" while Shorter's "Footprints" and "Infant Eyes" are gems from his classic Blue Note albums. Shorter then spent fifteen years co-leading the fusion group Weather Report and recording Brazilian jazz. Hancock created a jazz-funk sound (*Mwandishi, Headhunters*), and later, the hiphopped electro-funk of "Rock It" (*Future Shock*, 1983).

When Miles Davis went electric (1969-74), it was as controversial within jazz as Bob Dylan's heretical move four years earlier. His musical epiphany was *electric-meets-acoustic:* he discovered that acoustic horns balance well with and against electric pianos, guitars, and basses. His first attempt was *In a Silent Way*, a late-night atmospheric masterpiece that anticipates ambient, electronica, and chill lounge music. There was one 20-minute jam per side featuring an expanded ensemble with electric guitar (John McLaughlin) and two electric pianos (Hancock and Chick Corea). "Shhh/ Peaceful" is the aural equivalent of watching a quiet storm move across the night sky —that is, if the clouds were colorized and set off occasional lavender flashes of heat lightning. "In a Silent Way" is a three-part suite that starts with a sunrise: the first movement rises slowly on the wings of ethereal trumpet and soprano saxophone lines as they skim over a rippling electric guitar and low waves of electric piano. The trumpet kicks off a more urgent tempo at the four-minute mark, starting the second movement. Layers of synth carry the groove while guitar and bass create internal turbulence and build rhythmic tension. Then the first movement is repeated for five minutes of complex serenity.

Bitches Brew then created a system break in jazz history. There are eleven musicians here and the dominant sound is of a lush electric underbrush with acoustic horns diving into and out of the mix. McLaughlin's guitar agitates the electric pianos in side-battles, Davis' trumpet floats in to make announcements, the bass clarinet thickens the percussive mix. "Miles Runs The Voodoo Down" unfolds through gradual tempo shifts and slow crescendos, clustered rhythmic entanglements, and piercing trumpet solos. *Voodoo* works as a multi-layered metaphor here: there is the en-*trance*ment of repetition and variation, the decoding of secrets, the illumination of dark truths. Davis' opening and closing solos create structure and at key moments, his streaming hornlines slice open the orchestral pudding.

Davis idolized boxers and honored the first black heavyweight champion with *A Tribute to Jack Johnson*. The album links Davis' phrasing to Johnson's ring mastery, creating an analogy of his musical phrasing to jabs and sonic punches. Again, there are two half-hour jams. On "Right Off", there is an assertive amped-up power: McLaughlin's blues-rock riff locks in with drummer Billy Cobham's driving pulse to support Davis's electrified trumpet. The electric guitar spits blues chords at Davis, who hoovers up the electricity then shoots back galvanized trumpet blasts. "Yesternow", in contrast, begins as mood music for a vacation on the moon with its loping seven-note bassline and Hancock's organ riffs. A soprano sax solo builds to a climax at the halfway mark and the piece breaks off into a funkier and more abrasive second movement.

Davis stopped recording for six years after his electric period. During this period of substance abuse, hedonism, and lost purpose, the fusion torch passed to his musicians. John McLaughlin's Mahavishnu Orchestra created a heavy-metal jazz rock with grand themes alluding to Eastern religions. Its sound was heavier than the Davis units, thicker in its electricity, more vaunted in projecting power, and devoid of horns for acoustic moderation. Chick Corea and Return to Forever featured many Davis alumni yet its albums often feature an excess of electrical noodling and lack the innovative textures of Davis's records.

An exception is Return to Forever's *Light as a Feather,* a fusion masterpiece. Spanish motifs, brilliant melodies, and Brazilian rhythms combine as if there's an open door at the beach-house and an all-star jazz band is practicing next door. Buoyed by Airto Moreira's Brazilian percussion, Corea's solos on the Fender Rhodes ("500 Miles High"), Clarke's bubbling basslines, and Joe Farrell's flute, Brazilian vocalist Flora Purim sails through the title track and "You're Everything". Corea began his career in Latin big bands and, like Miles Davis, he was fascinated by Spain's classical music.

Miles Davis guided jazz along in its century-long mission as a crucible for creative genre synergies. Jazz remains the primordial river of American music taking in all the streams, now including EDM, DJ sound sculptures, ambient music, and hiphop.

John Coltrane: Excavations of the Spirit

John Coltrane was considered a spiritual leader in the 1960s by younger musicians and fans; there is even a ministry in his name, the Saint John Coltrane Church in San Francisco. As musically restless as Miles Davis, Coltrane shifted from exhaustively inventive solos to next-level quartet conversation to prayerful keening wails. He also explored the relationship between musical structures and mathematical concepts. Footage of his extended solos frame a man seemingly trying to reach God through his saxophone.

To "Trane", every chord contained a musical universe. With the Miles Davis Quintet, he often seemed to play every possible variation of the chord in each solo. Once in rehearsal, Miles waited impatiently for him to finish a long solo. "I just don't know how to stop", Trane told his boss sheepishly. Miles' deadpan reply: "Take the horn out of your mouth". Yet their opposite aesthetic styles were key to the quartet's success: Trane was the heated, passionate soloist following Davis' cool Romantic minimalism; Davis' trumpet was a narrating voice, Coltrane's tenor a blasting stick. Even while in The Miles Davis Quintet, Coltrane explored new depths in the blues and African music (*Blue Train, Bahia)* until his heroin addiction got him fired.

Embarrassed by losing his dream job, Coltrane quit cold turkey and within six months released his first classic, *Giant Steps*. "Giant Steps" and "Countdown" showcase his "sheets of sounds" approach, raining down torrents of notes for each chord change, showing his mastery of European harmony as played with split-second, exhausting creativity. There is also a beautiful ballad, "Naima", an ode to his first wife, and "Spiral", a mid-tempo ballad built of descending chords that actually creates a sonic sense of spiraling.

Over a five year period (1960-1964), Coltrane recorded more than a dozen albums, evenly divided between accessible and experimental works. When critics called his more dissonant works "anti-jazz", his record label countered with restrained lyrical albums of standards: *Ballads, John Coltrane and Duke Ellington, John Coltrane and Johnny Hartman*. During this period, he explored raga patterns in classical Indian music (the 14-minute "India"), the musical modes of Islamic Spain (the 18-minute "Ole"), and African polyrhythms (on *Africa/Brass)*. "I like to play long", he once said and these epic pieces cracked open bebop's *theme-solos-theme* format for younger musicians. The young saxophonist Archie Shepp learned long-form improvisation from Coltrane and that "we had to have the stamina —in terms of imagination and physical preparedness— to sustain these long flights".

A few albums were accessible *and* innovative, such as *Impressions* and *My Favorite Things* (1961).

Four years before *The Sound of Music* became a hit film, Coltrane recorded this 13-minute meditation, instantly familiar as a song and also as art. He had picked up the soprano saxophone and its higher sound lightened his intensity; Coltrane had always reached for the highest notes on the tenor and now here was a higher range at his fingertips. Pianist McCoy Tyner moderates his flights with tremolos that flow like a calming fountain.

The Coltrane Quartet's Controlled Chaos

In the early 1960s, the John Coltrane Quartet was the model for jazz's exploratory equilibrium due to its internal synergy: Tyner's shimmering waves on piano are steadied by Jimmy Garrison's breathing pulse; the percussive whirlwind of Elvin Jones' drumming creates its own gulf stream with Coltrane at the center. The quartet was like a sonic manifestation of the atomic symbol: a dynamic, roiling, self-contained system of ongoing multiple fissions.

All the quartet's strengths are on display on the superb *Live at Birdland*. With Coltrane and Jones often dueling, bassist Jimmy Garrison controls and drives the tempo. On "Afro Blue", Coltrane plies the highest range of the soprano sax while Jones splashes cymbals and rumbles around the drum set, creating polyrhythms. Coltrane's stirring solo on "I Want To

Talk About You" transforms this standard's beautiful melody into a lyrical concerto and when it seemingly ends after five minutes, Coltrane is simply not done: then for three minutes, he plays perhaps the most rapturous solo cadenza in jazz.

Then comes "Alabama" —a poignant dirge recorded only three months after the murder of four little girls in a Birmingham church. Coltrane here mediates the grief of African-Americans stunned by this act of racial hatred. He stays in the lower register of the tenor —unusual for him— and it sounds like a preacher's deep voice. This was intentional: Coltrane tried to reflect the cadences of Martin Luther King, Jr., a rare example of vocalizing an instrument to reflect a specific person.

"Alabama" begins with Tyner slowly rolling octaves like an approaching storm and Coltrane offers short, oratorical phrases of dignified grieving. The hymn seems to end quickly (@1:40) —but then Coltrane blows three slow, bent notes as if of a broken heart, falling into the rhythm section's arms. The quartet then re-states the theme and finds a mid-tempo groove, as if leading the congregation in mourning. A minute later, the song suddenly halts again, as if Trane cannot find the words to continue (2:40). He re-begins tentatively while the bass searches for stable emotional ground. The hymn seems to end a third time (4:25) but then Coltrane opens up a quick seam of grief with a high, pealing line that descends just as quickly into the quiet, fading thunder of the tom-toms.

Joel Dinerstein

QIJ - NYC

Created by Joel Dinerstein · 29 songs, 4 hr 9 min

PLAY

FOLLOWERS 0

Download

TITLE	ARTIST	ALBUM		
Miles Runs the Voodoo Down	Miles Davis	Bitches Brew	2020-04-23	14:01
Right Off	Miles Davis	A Tribute To Jack Johns…	2020-04-23	26:54
You're Everything	Chick Corea, Return To…	Light As A Feather	2020-04-23	5:11
My Favorite Things	John Coltrane	My Favorite Things	2020-04-23	13:44
I Want To Talk About You - Live At Birdland, NY…	John Coltrane	1963: New Directions	2020-04-23	8:12
Alabama - Live At Birdland Jazzclub, New York…	John Coltrane	Live At Birdland	2020-04-23	5:09
Wise One	John Coltrane Quartet	Crescent	2020-04-23	9:04
A Love Supreme, Pt. I – Acknowledgement	John Coltrane	A Love Supreme	2020-04-23	7:43
Lovely Sky Boat	Alice Coltrane	A Monastic Trio	2020-04-23	6:55
The Creator Has A Master Plan	Pharoah Sanders	Karma	2020-04-23	32:47
Lonely Woman	Ornette Coleman	The Shape Of Jazz To …	2020-04-23	5:02
3 Wishes	Ornette Coleman, Jerr…	Virgin Beauty	2020-04-23	4:19

6. Dinerstein's New York City playlist, 2.

The next year, Coltrane's musical quest was eclipsed by his spiritual inquiry: *Crescent* was the quartet's last album of soulful exploration while *A Love Supreme* was a religious vision rendered in sound. *Crescent* sustains a dark meditative mood with mostly long ballads: its first two tracks are exemplary models of jazz beauty —Crescent" and "Wise One"— through Coltrane's scalar explorations of melody, the intelligence of Tyner's solos, and Jones' cymbal washes. "Lonnie's Lament" features a beautiful opening theme and a compelling five-minute bass solo. Jones takes a freeform seven-minute solo on "The Drum Thing" that suggests hidden African drum ensembles. "Bessie's Blues" is the only uptempo track, a hard bop tribute to blues singer Bessie Smith with an innovative twist on the standard 12-bar blues. *Crescent* feels like both an elegy and a spirit-raising, an album in full consciousness of the African diaspora.

A Love Supreme is an iconic masterpiece, Coltrane's religious vision in four parts. The album is a praise song for God's creation yet it connected with political activists, Black workers, hippies, and two generations of musicians. It blew open the doors of musical perception for Carlos Santana, Jerry Garcia, and Joni Mitchell, and later, for Patti Smith and Steely Dan, Bono and Peter Buck. The suite enfolds a generation of jazz creativity through bebop and hard bop, blues and gospel shouts, African drumming and European harmony. Like many jazz classics of the

1960s, *A Love Supreme* was recorded at Rudy Van Gelder's studio just outside New York in suburban Englewood Cliffs, New Jersey.

"Part I: Acknowledgment" works through ostinatos (repetitions) of a short blues phrase: Coltrane explores the loping four-note motif from every side then ends with the chant, "a love supreme". "Part II: Resolution" opens with a memorable melody line that leaps upward and Coltrane enjoys the half-step descent back to center each time, blasting off four times before ceding musical ground to Tyner's two-minute solo. Coltrane re-enters (3:54) with new energy until he distorts the tenor's sound as if trying to wrestle entirely new chords from the saxophone (5:33-6:33). "Part III: Pursuance" is almost literal: this fast, intense section suggests that you can chase God all you want but will not catch Him. Garrison's thoughtful, mournful bass solo ends the chase and the quartet transitions softly into the opening measures of the final movement.

"Part IV: Psalm" is an instrumental recitation of a poem printed in the album's liner notes. It is a collective prayer, freely played on only one chord. The poem's first line might be the album's theme, "I will do all I can to be worthy of Thee O Lord". The satisfying sonic contrast comes from the low rumbling on tympani as Coltrane ascends until he runs out of horn. The poem's most telling line, "We are alone in His grace", highlights a paradox of the quartet, each musician "alone" but creating a larger state of collective grace.

Coltrane left all musical structure behind (and many of his fans) with *Ascension* (1965) —it will sound like an irredeemable cacophony to some and an ear-blowing experience to others. Then with *Meditations* (1966), he even left his quartet behind. Tyner and Jones could not identify their own musical voices within these dense, powerful unrhythmic layers of free improvisation. Tyner heard inchoate noise and could not hear how he might contribute to this new sound. Elvin Jones was suspicious of music without a tempo and took offense when Coltrane hired a second drummer. Coltrane's wife, Alice, became the new pianist; saxophonist Pharoah Sanders became his closest musical partner.

Coltrane's unexpected death of liver cancer stunned the jazz community in 1967. Alice Coltrane carried on his vision: she recorded a tribute album on piano and harp with her husband's rhythm section (*A Monastic Trio*). The startling sound of the harp brings an entirely new sound to jazz: in "Lovely Sky Boat" and "Oceanic Beloved", wave after wave of chimed light fill the air, its sonic qualities reminiscent of the West African kora. The trio tracks are dark and moody, either bluesy and diffuse or religious and celebratory ("Gospel Trane"). She delved deeper into Indian classical music and religion than her husband, moving to an ashram and founding a center for the study of Vedic scripture. Her classic collaboration with Pharoah Sanders, *Journey In Satchidananda*, registers as a Zen jazz album with her harp resounding against the *tanpura*, an Indian drone instrument. If this album now sounds like yoga music, that is due more to its success than New Age superficialities.

Pharoah Sanders utilized the tenor as a prophesying instrument as on his masterpiece, the 32-minute musical mandala, "The Creator Has a Master Plan". Sanders started out in Oakland R&B bands and you can hear that big, rocking sax style at the base of his tenor's deep kettle sound. He plays an opening ostinato for two minutes then quotes a motif from *A Love Supreme*. For six minutes, it settles into a pastoral foundation of flutes, tambourine, and hand percussion, while Sanders mixes stentorian blues statements with smeared waves of sound. The band often just vamps, creating a relaxing feeling up until vocalist Leon Thomas chants, "The creator has a working plan / peace and happiness for every man" (@8:00). Thomas warbles until he wails; Sanders bellows deeply until he starts to shriek. The music is spiritual, angry, and in search of harmony, reflecting the decade's rage and racial upheavals. This is music for brave sonic souls and not for the faint of heart or ear.

The John Coltrane Quartet distilled jazz history to that moment into four instruments: the drums represented Africa and its multiple heritages; the piano, Europe and its classical legacy; the saxophone was a twentieth-century American expressive instrument; the bass was also a new instrument, its flexibility for creating new grooves a far cry from its carnival beginnings. The quartet format was now capable of jazz's entire range: conversation, propulsion, orchestral density; elegy, prayer, dance, concerto; raga, blues, standard, global rhythms.

Ornette Coleman Frees Jazz

Ornette Coleman's alto sound is both primal *and* experimental. He seems to scratch blues skronk out of a gritty, sandy windstorm —suggesting a wolf's cry, the blues tradition of his home state of Texas, and even the fragmentation of society. His first gig at the Five Spot divided the jazz community in 1958: his quartet bypassed bebop's chord changes and Ornette played a white plastic alto saxophone! Coleman created the post-bebop revolution of *free jazz* and he is jazz's most influential avant-garde composer. Saxophonist Joe Zawinul distilled Coleman's work into a useful four-word mantra: "Nobody solos, everybody solos".

Coleman's third album was a manifesto —*The Shape of Jazz to Come*— and it codified free jazz: the structure was open-ended, the soloing free-associative, the rhythm section loose in its guidance; there were few chords. The music was both meditative and gritty, soulful and *a*-tonal (that is, off the Western scale). The album now has two jazz standards: "Lonely Woman", a ballad of pensive sorrow and blue shavings, and "Peace", in which Charlie Haden's earthy pulse balances the dissonant hornlines. There are many free-form duets of Coleman's alto and Haden's bass, as if they represent two *musical* tramps in a free jazz version of Samuel Beckett's *Waiting for Godot*. Concurrent with Beckett's work during the Cold War, Coleman's early albums offer the lonely wail, the blank canvas, voice and witness, the stripping of an art form down to its primal elements.

In short, Coleman de-centered jazz: his music is centrifugal rather than centripetal. His music partakes of *polyphony* —multiple lines— akin to New Orleans music but freed of all chords, keys, and structures. Coleman's vision transcended the core objective of most composed music, the alternation of tension and release. In free jazz, each musician continually shifts position to find the right spaces to create the most dynamic effects. By *New York Is Now!* (1968), Coltrane's former rhythm section seemed more comfortable with Coleman's free jazz and the album appeared on jazz's foremost record label, Blue Note.

Still one often hears the joy in his adventurous melodies, as on "Congeniality" or "Beauty Is A Rare Thing". Between 1960-75, Coleman wrote a symphony, recorded with the legendary Master Musicians of Jajouka, and integrated jazz with North African "desert music". Like Miles Davis, he began experimenting with electric instruments and it, too, led Coleman to a revolutionary conception. He created a new musical theory, *harmolodics*: as the name suggests, equal value is placed on harmony, melody, rhythm, and sound movement.

Coleman first went electric with *Dancing In Your Head* (1975), a cacophonous mix of North African ethnic rhythms, folk motifs, and free-form funk. Coleman's acoustic wailings abrasively mesh with electric guitars while the rhythm section kicks in different directions until the band falls together in the last section. The music is analogous to the compositions of Philip Glass or Steve Reich, if more dissonant, as all three composers prioritized rhythmic texture over melody and harmony.

By 1982's *Of Human Feelings,* Coleman and his band Prime Time had developed harmolodics into profoundly complex funk. Coleman doubled rock's power-trio format with two electric guitarists, two electric bassists and two drummers. Yet there is a compelling warmth within the crunching interplay of guitarist James Blood Ulmer, bassist Jamaladeen Tacuma, and drummer Calvin Weston. On "Jump Street", Coleman's riff drops into the bassline and the band generates a dense rhythmic bandwidth roiling with new colors and patterns. Halfway through comes a harmolodic epiphany: the musicians break free, the guitars take their lines in opposites directions, the drummers sizzle, and Coleman plays into the funk as if kicking over a bonfire until all its elements have burned off.

Coleman enjoyed a plateau of artistic fulfillment in the 1980s, including two albums with unlikely guitarists: *Song X* (with Pat Metheny) and *Virgin Beauty* (with Jerry Garcia). *Song X* features tricky, intricate melodies with Metheny's guitar synthesizer adding a fusion element while Coleman also plays violin and trumpet. *Virgin Beauty* is an accessible, funky, atmospheric masterpiece. The album is a chugging, cerebral ride across the desert, with buoyant basslines and juicy internal guitar riffs. On the uptempo Coleman/Garcia tracks, they enjoy the happy convergence of groove-driven souls ("3 Wishes", "Desert Players"); on the ballads, Coleman's alto is more soulful than shredding, a bridge between cultures ("Healing the Feeling", "Unknown Artist"). The title track is a crackling desert late twilight as the stars rise in the night sky.

Perhaps the best route into harmolodics is Prime Time's version of the *Prelude* from Bach's *Cello Suite #1*. The band first plays it straight with the electric guitar carrying the melody with a certain stateliness, bumped along by tabla, synth, and percussion. The climax of the original takes about ten seconds, there is a momentary fade-out (@ 2:27-2:40), and then the band explodes into a starburst of sound: Coleman's alto spray-paints a mandala that takes shape right before your ears. Prime Time creates a pulsating jazz heart at the center of a Bach prelude while keeping the melody at the center of its swirling rhythmic vortex.

Since the 1990s, young jazz fans often find their way to free jazz after encounters with punk, death metal, industrial music, or atonality. Coleman's music broke open sound barriers such that musicians and listeners now easily hear its melodies, freedom, and profound funk.

From New York to New Musics

Bebop transformed jazz into an art of self-expression, as Gato Barbieri recalls from his apprenticeship. The Argentinian saxophonist had his first epiphanies listening to Coltrane and Ornette Coleman in the early 1960s: "[I] wanted very much to be a black jazz musician", he reflected. But he soon desired a sound that reflected his *own* cultural roots, the story of "another part of the world where there is great oppression". Barbieri found his own musical ground in Argentinian folk rhythms at live performances of tango musicians, who he found "tell their stories [with] the same power, feeling, and spontaneity" as jazz musicians. By 1970, jazz had become both a method and a music.

Max Roach called Dizzy Gillespie "the Gatherer", and two generations later, young trumpeter Roy Hargrove echoed this sentiment: "We're all his [Dizzy's] children and he lives on in us". Miles Davis spent five years withdrawn into substance abuse until Gillespie rebuked him: "God had given him a great gift, and if he didn't use it God was going to take it back". Davis started recording and playing again. "Dizzy was my God", trumpeter Jon Faddis once said, "and I will try to keep his spirit alive by helping other young musicians the way he helped me". The last band Gillespie formed was the United Nations Orchestra and he packed it with jazz musicians from Latin America and the Caribbean.

Miles, Coltrane, and Ornette influenced '60s rock-and-roll in several ways. The Byrds' "Eight Miles High" was directly inspired by Coltrane's modal albums, *Impressions* and *Africa/Brass* —you can hear it in the intro and guitar solo. Guitarist Rob Krieger of the Doors heard in Coltrane's "My Favorite Things" the kind of vamping he brought to the band's eight-minute "Light My Fire". He challenged Jim Morrison, "This freedom, this improvisation in jazz —how do we get it into rock'n'roll?" Guitarist Duane Allman's melodic phrasing was indebted to *Kind of Blue*: "I've listened to that album so many times that for the past couple of years, I haven't hardly listened to anything else". In the 1960s, Lou Reed recalled, "I used to run around the Village following Ornette Coleman wherever he played".

Yet jazz musicians received little official recognition until the 1990s. Duke Ellington was denied a Pulitzer Prize citation in 1965 when two judges resigned rather than award it to a Black man. "Fate doesn't want me to be too famous too young", he said with characteristic diplomacy. Three decades later, the first Pulitzer awarded to an extended jazz composition went to trumpeter Wynton Marsalis for *Blood on the Fields* (1997). Like Miles Davis, Marsalis left Julliard —he signed up with Art Blakey and the Messengers along with his brother, saxophonist Branford Marsalis. Within two years, each musician started his own band and Blakey replaced them with Terence Blanchard (trumpet) and Donald Harrison (sax). All four musicians were born-and-raised in New Orleans.

Yet the Marsalises' neo-traditionalism was offset by the eclectic downtown scene, a rich ferment of new jazz directions. There is a palpable spirit of experimentation and exploding sonic barriers in these bands. New clubs in Tribeca supported this eclectic scene of mutual influence such as Tonic, Roulette, and the Knitting Factory: it included the bossa nova punk jazz of Arto Lindsay, the collagist jazz funk of bassist Bill Laswell, the post-Ornette shredded guitar sound of Sonny Sharrock, and the reimagined hard bop of the David Murray Octet. The depth of Cassandra Wilson's vocal aesthetic comes from her work with Henry Threadgill and others, long before she created an accessible synthesis of funk, jazz, delta blues, pop, country, and world rhythms (*New Moon Daughter*, *Blue Light 'Til Dawn*).

John Zorn seemed to be everywhere as altoist, impresario, producer, and club owner. He explored the outer reaches of improvisational noise in the 1980s then reigned in his radical improvisation in Naked City. Since 2000, he has created an epic project of avant-garde ethnic Jewish music, *Book of Angels*: Zorn conducts his own compositions, a mix of klezmer, minor-key Jewish folk melodies, chamber music, Middle Eastern rhythms, rock flourishes, and free jazz dissonance.

Like Zorn, David Murray was ubiquitous in 1980s/90s New York as co-leader of the World

Saxophone Quartet (WSQ) and leader of his own Octet. In Murray's saxophone sound, a listener hears everyone from Coleman Hawkins to Dexter Gordon to Coltrane to Pharoah Sanders, and he is a master balladeer. The Octet was a band of young all-stars whose internal cross-harmonies rivaled harmolodics on acoustic instruments with complex ballads ("Ming", "Jasvan"). The WSQ is a blues-shouting free jazz quartet of tenor, soprano, alto, and baritone saxophones, and it brought Black popular music genres back home to jazz (*Rhythm & Blues, Dances & Ballads*). An expatriate living in Paris, Murray is one of the most important musicians of the past half-century through his standards quartet, tributes to Nat King Cole and the Grateful Dead, and albums with African drummers.

Ornette Coleman achieved official recognition late in life —a MacArthur Genius Grant in 1994 and a Pulitzer for *Sound Grammar* (2006)— but enjoyed a more evocative tribute in 2014 at "Celebrate Ornette" in Brooklyn's Prospect Park. With a house harmolodic band led by drummer Denardo Coleman (his son), a cross-section of New York's music scene showed how his music had diffused into the global soundscape. The saxophones of Sonny Rollins, David Murray, John Zorn, and Henry Threadgill blended with post-punk guitarists James Blood Ulmer, Thurston Moore, and Nels Cline. Patti Smith recited a tribute, tap-dancer Savion Glover added rhythm, Laurie Anderson played violin drones with the

Master Musicians of Joujouka. Everyone soloed on "Blues Connotation" to create a dissonant orchestral swirl that was at-once harmonic, polyvocal, kinetic, dynamic, and medicinally chaotic. Ornette always said he was "pro-sound" and welcomed it all.

Chapter 5

Los Angeles: West Coast Jazz Connections

In 1945, jazz audiences in Los Angeles crowded into Billy Berg's club to see Bird and Diz, the prophets of bebop. Many jazz fans drifted away due to the new idiom's angular rhythms, extended solos, and harmonic complexities —but for the musicians, Parker's arrival was an epiphany. Pianist Hampton Hawes and altoist Sonny Criss, both teenagers, had conversion experiences: Criss had a new idol; "I was molded on the spot", Hawes said, "like a piece of clay stamped out. Parker stayed for a year on his next visit and the two young musicians often played alongside him in Central Avenue clubs while Bird often stayed with the young trumpeter Art Farmer.

When Parker returned to LA for a gig in 1952, he hired Chet Baker, a white trumpeter with a mellow romantic thrust, to complement his edgier harmonic runs. Within a few short years, Chet Baker became a pop-cultural icon. His dreamy melodic sound, chiseled beauty, heroin addiction, and rebel persona —all combined to make him jazz's charismatic white anti-hero, the James Dean of jazz. As rebels, Baker and Parker were both unapologetic heroin addicts focused solely on their own musical artistry. When Parker returned to New York he told musicians, "I met a little white cat who's gonna wipe you out".

"West Coast jazz" is an umbrella term for jazz's last regional style and some of its musical traits are *very* laid-back LA: relaxed tempos, cool sonorities, waves of melody, light swing, fluid solos, soft Latin rhythms. In LA, there was more emphasis put on song structures and unusual voicings —such as the piano-less quartet of Baker and baritone saxophonist Gerry Mulligan. In comparison to New York's hard bop —with its passion, protest, and long solos— LA musicians stuck closer to the melody and swung lightly. There is aural space around each instrument and, depending on one's imagination, the ambience of sun, ocean, and beach. This quick sketch applies to saxophonists Art Pepper, Paul Desmond, Zoot Sims, and Harold Land, trumpeters Art Farmer and Shorty Rogers, guitarist Jim Hall, and clarinetist Jimmy Giuffre.

West Coast jazz was once considered a white musical style, but this mistaken idea ignored several social factors: inter-racial bands, shared musical influences, Latin rhythms, the common use of heroin, the common experience of prison. LA musicians shared four musical lodestars at mid-century: for solos, Charlie Parker's speed and harmonic complexity; for tonal colors, Duke Ellington and arranger Gil Evans; for sound and style, Lester Young's melodic imagination; for swinging equilibrium, the Count Basie rhythm section. A few New York legends even blossomed during periods of West Coast residency (e.g., Ornette Coleman, Charlie Haden, Max Roach).

The LA scene begins on Central Avenue, the center of Black business and nightlife in South Los Angeles. Any given night on "The Avenue" in small clubs, you might find bassist Charles Mingus with the "Stars of Swing", T-Bone Walker creating his brand of jazzy blues guitar, or Nat King Cole playing swing piano before his singing career took off. Dexter Gordon was the Avenue's hip young lion in the 1940s, a towering six-foot-five tenor saxophonist and an icon of cool from jazz photography. White musicians were welcome: alto saxophonist Art Pepper was in drummer Lee Young's band as a 14-year-old! The Central Avenue scene faded in the 1950s, due to police harassment of inter-racial socializing and the heroin scourge.

In the late 1960s, the CTI label created something of a "California sound" featuring lush production, light funk, and a pop sensibility. Its opposite number was the community jazz of Horace Tapscott's Pan-

Afrikan Peoples Arkestra, a big band that played solely at local South LA venues. Tapscott alumni David Murray and Arthur Blythe moved to New York and became major forces on its downtown scene. More recently, jazz, hiphop, and electronica have meshed in LA, creating a jazz future for young audiences around DJ Flying Lotus, guitarist Thundercat, and saxophonist Kamasi Washington.

Cool Jazz in California:
Chet Baker & Gerry Mulligan

New York's legendary *Birth of the Cool* sessions were a bi-coastal project and the big bang of West Coast jazz. The first partnership of Miles Davis and Gil Evans, the compositions were "through-composed" rather than improvised, as in bebop's *theme-solos-theme* format. Each song was arranged and scored with individual sections and learned parts, leaving room for only one or two short solos; piano and drums were de-emphasized. This mixture of jazz and classical music was called "third-stream music" in the 1950s: some found it a melodic relief from bebop's avant-garde intensity while others found it boring.

Baritone saxophonist Gerry Mulligan was the third architect of the cool sessions, writing and arranging three of its tracks. When he moved to California in 1950, he continued thinking along the same lines: lighter tone, muted horns, more structure, shorter solos (less blowing). At his own gigs, Mulligan enjoyed swinging without a piano and found that the horns relaxed (the drums, too) when liberated from the hold of this venerable instrument.

Mulligan had a residency at a small club called The Haig and Chet Baker often showed up at jam sessions. Baker's sweet, higher tone was a perfect foil for the hollow-bodied call of the baritone sax. Mulligan and Baker thrilled audiences with their improvised countermelodies, two voices building an aural helix. In one way, the unusual pairing of trumpet and bari sax refreshed the original New Orleans front-line dueling of trumpet and clarinet; in another, the conversational quality of the quartet echoed Billie Holiday's chamber jazz. When recording, Mulligan insisted on an "integrated group sound" with all instruments mixed at the same volume.

In "Frenesi", Mulligan opens with a short ascending melodic riff, Baker's trumpet quickly echoes it an octave higher, they repeat the solo lines, and drummer Chico Hamilton's *castanet-ish* Latin rhythm joins them together. The bass enters to balance the quartet and we have four equal voices happily swinging, with congas added for percussive color. Mulligan's solo emerges organically, backed only by the drummer's crisp brushwork. A Latin interlude follows that launches Baker's spare, measured solo while the cymbals shimmer. Baker's trumpet brings melodic clarity to the Latin motif towards the end, Mulligan counters, and the rhythm section skitters out on the fade.

The piano-less Mulligan-Baker quartet became an instant star attraction with a best-selling album. But within a year, Mulligan was arrested for heroin possession and served six months in jail. In his absence, Chet Baker became a singer and a *bona fide* pop star.

You can hear why on the hit "Let's Get Lost". This is jazz as urbane pop music and the song works through four discrete one-minute sections in a listener's mind. First, Baker introduces the melody in a set of exchanges with the piano. The surprise comes in the second minute with Baker's high, soft, distinctive, off-kilter vocal style: he mixes an internal rhythmic sense with the artistic capacity to ignore it. The third minute is Baker's solo, a deep exploration of the melody accented by the cymbals, followed by a short piano solo. In the final minute, "let's get lost" becomes "let's de*frost* / in a romantic mist" —delivered slightly under-pitch— as if he hopes love is something like heroin. Such tonal breaks transform the song into a lived short story —much like Sinatra and Billie Holiday— while the mixture of toughness and vulnerability reflected the new young masculinity of the 1950s.

Unlike New York's beboppers, LA musicians such as Mulligan remained more invested in "the depth and profundity of big band music", Art Farmer recalled. "My first ambition was just to be a member of that sound in a big band. I would have been very happy just to be the second or third trumpet player [in a section]". Farmer was not a soloist at first, but with the bebop turn, "to stay in [the] music you had to be able to play a decent solo". LA musicians created a synthesis of bebop and big band swing, leading to the city's many big small band projects: *Gerry Mulligan and His Tentette*, *Art Pepper + Eleven*, the *Art Farmer-Benny Golson Jazztet*.

The Jazztet's upbeat "It's All Right With Me", for example, depends upon its two musical rows: a front line of horns (trumpet, trombone, saxophone) and a rhythm section back line (piano, bass, and drums). Carried along by the fast-tempo on the high-hat and cymbals, the melody evokes a train arriving at the station where lovers long parted sweep into a speeding cab. Inflections of the reunion are carried through the changing moods of the solos. The romantic tryst peaks with Curtis Fuller's stand-out trombone solo —then quick two-measure drum fills cheer the lovers on, phrases echoed by a young McCoy Tyner on piano. This is a joyful jazz performance for all seasons.

The LA scene thrived on experimentation with such new voicings. Nat King Cole's first trio started as a quartet but the drummer failed to appear for the first gig. Cole so enjoyed the easy swing with just the guitar comping and the bass bumping the groove along, he shifted to a trio, The King Cole Swingsters. This lighter sound still seems to match the cultural imagination of a laid-back California sound.

On the Avenue: Dexter Gordon and Charles Mingus

For young LA musicians, Central Avenue was apprenticeship and finishing school all rolled into one. "The Avenue" was a long strip of clubs, hotels, theaters, and restaurants, along with gambling and prostitution —akin to Harlem's 125th St. or Chicago's Stroll. Billie Holiday or Cab Calloway might be playing at upscale venues such as the Dunbar Hotel or Club Alabam; there were jam sessions at the Downbeat and Ivie's Chicken Shack; after-hours, there was Jack's Basket Room, owned by boxing champion Jack Johnson. KC blues singers Big Joe Turner and Julia Lee were rhythm-and-blues hitmakers *on the Avenue*, as was Charles Brown with his mellow jazzy piano blues.

Dexter Gordon and Charles Mingus both grew up in Watts, a vibrant multi-ethnic neighborhood with integrated public schools. Los Angeles was a target city of the Great Migration and new settlers came for jobs in the defense industries. Watts offered a countrified space in the city where White, Black, Mexican, and Japanese families often built their own homes. Mingus and "Dex" both went to Jefferson High School and studied under legendary music teacher Samuel Browne, whose high-school swing band also featured Sonny Criss, Art Farmer, drummer Chico Hamilton, R&B star Big Jay McNeely, and arranger Melba Liston. Many Jefferson High graduates later played in the Los Angeles City

College band, something of a minor-league team for big bands filling up their sections.

Gordon often engaged fellow saxophonist Wardell Gray in 20-minute tenor battles on "The Hunt", whether in front of a thousand fans at the Elk's Club or Jack's Basket Room. "We were coming out of the same bag —Lester and Bird", Gordon recalled. Dexter synthesized Young, Parker, and Webster to create a big, deep, relaxed, soulful sound. His hip clique shared Bird and heroin to the extent that he hawked new bebop records to local barbershops, where men discussed politics and Parker's solos. In contrast, Mingus was the quintessential weird kid-turned-artist, a musical prodigy on bass who studied with classical teachers and always had composing on his mind.

Mingus and Gordon were at first innovating traditionalists: both musicians toured with Armstrong and loved Ellington, both followed Young's model of sound and swing at first, both absorbed Bird's changes. Gordon was socially and politically progressive: he worked and recorded with women such as trombonist/arranger Melba Liston and wrote "Blue Bikini" to protest the 1946 A-bomb tests on Bikini Atoll. Mingus honored his jazz mentors with tributes that rendered each man in style and personality: Ellington's elegance ("Open Letter to Duke"), Jelly Roll Morton's polyphonic imagination ("Jelly Roll"), Monk's pianistic twists ("Jump Monk"). Mingus' *memento mori* for Lester

Young —"Goodbye, Porkpie Hat"— remains the gold standard of jazz portraiture while Gordon left this poignant reflection, "Lester float[ed] in from some astral planet to steal our hearts and revolutionize our daily lives".

Gordon spent the 1950s in-and-out of prison for heroin possession. A joyful, swinging period followed celebrating Latin rhythms in "Soy Califa" (meaning "I am Californian"), churning out slow, erotic blues such as "Soul Sister", or on ballads such as "I Guess I'll Hang My Tears Out to Dry". Once clean, part of his healing came from acting: he portrayed an addict in a play (*The Connection)* and enjoyed acting. He composed music for the play then re-shaped it into the ballads of *Dexter Calling,* a classic album recorded with Miles Davis's rhythm section. Sick of racism, Gordon moved to Denmark in 1963 for fifteen years and enjoyed a quiet family life there.

Mingus' early compositional aesthetic was indebted to the LA sound, as represented on *Live at the Bohemia* (1955): here are the thematic structures, relaxed rhythms, and cooler sonorities of West Coast jazz. Mingus distilled Ellington's rich tonal blends and narrative pacing into a smaller combo while adding bebop's fluid virtuosity and complex harmonies. "Serenade In Blue" invokes Debussy's *La Mer* with its dark, dissonant horns until its pessimistic fog is dispelled by uplifting trombone and tenor solos. "Work Song" is a tribute to African-American workers, from railroads to chain gangs: the hammered tone-clusters on piano disrupt the ballad's rhythmic patterns at key moments as if to validate the workers' frustration at social injustice.

With the classic *Tijuana Moods*, Mingus redirected jazz's "Spanish tinges" to a Mexican context. With an LA-style front horn line of trumpet, sax and trombone, each composition swings through two-minute movements in shifting variations of tempo and mood linked either by solos or mellow interludes. The opener is "Dizzy Moods", a tribute to the inventor of Latin jazz (Gillespie), followed by "Los Mariachis", a tribute to how these musicians enliven public life. "Tijuana Gift Shop" is a sensual walk through the border city with Mingus' bass pulsating like blood through travelers' veins.

The centerpiece is "Ysabel's Table Dance", a ten-minute tone-poem that kicks off with a quick riff on castanets then mirrored on piano and bass. A female flamenco voice gathers the horns into an upward swirling vortex until it pops —musicians then lay low, rebuild the harmonies into near-cacophony, then resolve its tensions into a cool groove, spiked by soulful solos (2:00-3:00). This build-and-release structure is a Mingus signature and it works like a series of pressure valves: Ysabel's castanets lead to a hard-swinging riff, there is the slow crescendo into near-chaos, then an explosive pop and resolution, followed by a quiet interlude. Towards the end, the castanets play under swelling horn lines (7:00) until the flamenco singer returns with a few handclaps and a scratchy bass riff. This compositional approach informs his subsequent New York masterpiece, *Mingus Ah Um* (1959).

Gordon was a transitional figure dedicated to swinging even after absorbing bebop.

While living in Copenhagen, he became close friends with Ben Webster and inherited his saxophone when he died in 1973. He had been coasting for awhile and had a vivid dream of Webster sitting on his bed one night. "Hey, Dex, I hear you can't play anymore", Webster said, but Gordon disagreed with the apparition. "Well, if it's not true, prove it", Webster said, "Get up and start practicing". The dream scared Gordon to start practicing every day and getting back in top musical form.

Gordon made a triumphant return to New York in 1977 and, a decade later, became the public face of jazz's old guard with his Oscar-nominated performance in *Round Midnight* (1986). Gordon played aging saxophonist Dale Turner —based on Lester Young— and helped the director avoid clichés by changing the script's corny dialogue: "Jazz musicians don't talk like that", he often said. It remains the best feature film ever made about jazz musicians.

Like Gordon, many musicians from Central Avenue wound up in prison due to heroin possession —some lost their jazz footing, some were traumatized, some claimed police targeted musicians. The LAPD led the nation in narcotics arrests in the mid-1950s: the police weaponized incarceration to enforce an ideology of white supremacy. South LA residents resented the police as an occupying force —as well as the inferior public schools and hospitals of their communities— and their anger exploded in the Watts riots of 1965. Post-Watts, racial division separated the city's white and black musicians into different camps, reflecting the national schism of the Black Power and Black Arts movements in the 1960s.

Art Pepper and Frank Morgan: Altos, Addictions, Redemption

Altoists Art Pepper and Frank Morgan were child prodigies, lyrical balladeers, lifelong heroin addicts, fellow prisoners, and comeback kids. Both hung out and played on Central Avenue as teenagers and apprenticed in big bands, first imitating Young's lyricism then transformed by Bird and bebop. Pepper was a born rebel, arrogant and roguish, immersed in his music, sleazy towards his friends and women. The younger Morgan was naïve by comparison, mentored by trumpeter Clora Bryant, and a model prisoner. Pepper's career revived after the publication of *Straight Life* (1979), his classic memoir of jazz and heroin, while Morgan became one of jazz's finest balladeers in the 1980s.

At 15, Art Pepper was the alto in drummer Lee Young's sextet, soon enough hanging out and shooting up with Dex's hip clique. In his memoir, Pepper testifies to the generous and celebratory atmosphere on the Avenue as well as the presence of many white fans and musicians. After two years in the army, he returned and based his life on only two things: jazz and heroin. Pepper made his first solo records and consistently ranked second only to Bird in *Downbeat* polls as the best alto saxophonist.

One can hear why on "Blues In", a beautiful six-minute concerto from his classic album, *Modern Art* (1957). Pepper finds the sweet spot between the techniques of Young and Parker: his sinuous lyrical lines and effortless swing have a bluesy edge with surprising tonal breaks and sudden accelerated runs (1:50-2:10). Pepper shapes the air into an invisible sculpture of beauty, line, and imagination with only a bassist walking along for a bit of grounding. Yet he could burn rougher and faster, as with "Straight Life", his signature composition. Starting off at the breakneck pace Parker brought into jazz, Pepper pivots to take a few short, fast solos, then trades fours with the drummer in an impressive combination of atomic intensity and precision. This track appears on an album otherwise filled with lyrical versions of jazz standards such as "You'd Be So Nice to Come Home To" and "The Man I Love" (*Art Pepper Meets the Rhythm Section*, 1957).

By way of contrast, Frank Morgan was a shy, sensitive kid, a prodigy whose career in jazz was shaped by a chance meeting with Charlie Parker when he was seven years old. His father Stanley was a guitarist in the Ink Spots and knew Parker; he took his son to see KC's Jay McShann Orchestra in 1940 and its star soloist transformed young Frank's musical mind. Bird became Morgan's lifelong idol —a key presence in his life and the initial reason for his heroin addiction. Morgan was such an impressive Parker imitator at first that he was invited to join the Ellington Orchestra at 14. But his parents would not let him go on the road and instead he started his career as lead altoist in the house band of the Club Alabam.

A fascinating anecdote speaks to Morgan's talent, youth, and sensitivity during Billie Holiday's three-month residency at the Alabam. So deeply did Billie Holiday's vocal art affect the sensitive teenager that he often cried on the bandstand. A sharp entertainer, Holiday soon made it part of her performance: "Oh, there goes the little saxophonist again, he's crying again", she would say with sympathy. "Mama makes him cry every time".

Morgan made a solo album but his addiction soon led to thirty years of crime and prison. Jail time was moderated by jazz: he played in quartets and led the San Quentin big band, which included both Dex and Art Pepper in the 1950s. "San Quentin was filled with musicians from Central Avenue when I got there", he said. In the 1970s, the San Quentin All-Stars often sold out their Saturday night performances. Morgan remained off-the-radar until coming clean in 1985 and then became a major presence on New York's jazz scene.

Morgan treats notes as a poet does words, each one plumb with meaning that gather slowly into evocative phrases and colonize your mind. He also has a unique mastery of tempo that seems to slow down time itself, or at least the listener's relationship to it. In "Nefertiti", he holds a note for eight seconds (2:36), goes a step up in a different mood, then suddenly joyously segues into Ellington's "Don't Get Around Much Anymore". The tempo doubles and he steps into quickened bebop skeins punctuated with bent, expressive notes and crisp short phrases.

Morgan seems to be listening even when he's the only one talking. Sometimes he will double the tempo, fall out of it completely, cut it in half, or spiral free of it —all in the same solo. On "'Round Midnight", he rubs notes lightly, lyrically, sharply, darkly, passionately —he distorts a few, too, at worried moments or of seeming anger. This, too, makes his ballads seem like a raconteur's storytelling adapted to an attentive audience.

Morgan's life was a tribute to Parker's philosophy of music: "if you haven't lived it, it won't come out of your horn". Frank Morgan's delicate, crystalline sound holds the redemptive story of a sensitive kid, the allure of the alto, his struggle and self-rediscovery. This was equally true for Pepper, whose comeback occurred during a legendary four-night stand at New York's Village Vanguard in 1977. Charged up by Coltrane's drummer, Elvin Jones, the weekend was full of virtuosic performances that kicked off Pepper's rich final phase: two duet albums with pianist George Cables, one with strings, and the aptly-titled *Straight Life*. In Pepper's memoir, he expressed no remorse for his addiction or sleazy behavior; in fact, he allowed other voices to show him as a narcissistic, single-minded artist. For both altos, jazz was the saving grace of (straight) life itself.

The CTI Sound v. Horace Tapscott's Spiritual Community

In the 1970s, legendary jazz producer Creed Taylor helped create something of a "California sound" on the CTI label through a savvy combination of polished production, innovative rhythms, and marketing. CTI became identifiable through its integration of Latin and Brazilian rhythms, rock and funk, jazz guitar and the Fender Rhodes —all the decade's new jazz moves— into a set of pop sounds that left '60s protest in the rearview mirror. CTI's light funk and fusion, layered open space, atmospheric effects, and soulful horn solos fit the state's paradise vibe well enough to score hit records —from guitarist George Benson ("This Masquerade"), saxophonist Stanley Turrentine (*Sugar*), keyboardist Bob Jones ("Feel Like Making Love"), and Brazilian pianist Deodato (the theme from *2001: A Space Odyssey*).

Ironically, Taylor founded the Impulse! label in the 1960s —featuring the experimental soundscapes of Coltrane, Mingus, and Pharoah Sanders— yet only a few years later, he thought jazz could attract new audiences by meeting popular music halfway. He sanded jazz's rougher edges with strings and New Age spaciness; he gave the audience jazz funk and soul jazz for partying. Rather than standards, there were instrumental versions of popular hits: "California Dreamin'" (Benson), "Fire and Rain" (flutist Hubert Laws), "What's Going On" (Grover Washington, Jr.). CTI hired designers to create beautiful album covers and hired recording engineer Rudy Van Gelder away from the Blue Note label for his warm analog sound.

CTI also recorded the veteran artists of LA jazz: there was Chet Baker's comeback album, *She Was Too Good To Me* (1974), five albums by Art Farmer, and two classic albums from guitarist Jim Hall *(Big Blues* with Farmer, *Concierto* with Baker)*. On Chet Baker's "Funk in Deep Freeze", his melodic lead meshes with a walking electric bass and sustained chords on the Fender Rhodes, the recipe for CTI's light funk. A flute enters as a new voice and Baker dances with it (3:54 - 4:30) to elegant swinging. On "Whisper Not" (from *Big Blues*), Farmer's mellow flugelhorn runs interlock with Hall's tasteful chording against the unusual voicing of vibes, electric bass, and drums. CTI underscored its LA connection on its all-star live albums and compilations, such as *CTI Summer Jazz at the Hollywood Bowl* (1977).

CTI production may err on the slick side, but its house rhythm section were often Miles Davis alumni: Herbie Hancock, Ron Carter, and Jack DeJohnette. They were the foundation of Antonio Carlos Jobim's bossa nova albums and on trumpeter Freddie Hubbard's classic album, *Red Clay* (1971). The twelve-minute title track begins with a trumpet proclamation that leads to an orchestral constellation of sounds seemingly tuning up. The band then swings into the melody together before relaxing into a light funk groove from which solos emerge. "Delphia", the second track, features the unique voicing of trumpet and B3 organ —a gospel evocation— against blended horns that contrast Hubbard's sustained notes, sharp runs, and soulful gravitas. CTI's soul jazz division featured warm tenor saxophonists and funky organists partnered with young drummers such as Billy Cobham and Bernard Purdie.

One major criticism of the CTI sound focused on its *easy listening* sound —the label is one origin of "smooth jazz"— yet a redemption of sorts came in the 1990s when hiphop and neo-soul artists such as Erykah Badu, LL Cool J, and Snoop Dogg sampled the label's grooves. DJs and rappers cherish the CTI sound for its catchy riffs and clean production, its layered textures and Brazilian rhythms —all grist for the rapping mill and dancefloor. True to the '70s inter-racial jazz scene, white keyboardist Bob James is sampled as often as Black organist Johnny "Hammond" Smith. In retrospect, Creed Taylor simply had his finger on the pulse of jazz shifts and changing audience tastes.

Horace Tapscott's Community Leadership

Pianist Horace Tapscott's Pan-Afrikan People's Arkestra (PAPA) performed orchestral jazz in churches, parks, prisons, high schools, community centers, and coffee houses, mostly in South LA. Nearly always playing with young musicians and a 12-person choir, Tapscott's compositions were grand in sweep and dense in rhythmic texture, often featuring Afrofuturist tropes, as in "Niger's Theme" or "Little Africa". If CTI was a national brand, then Tapscott's objective was local knowledge focused on the objective of "preserving black music" as heritage and tradition. Tapscott's music was the sound of LA's urban facts on the ground: his objective seemed to be to represent his South LA community in sonic form.

Tapscott's music represents the last stand of the Central Avenue spirit. He played trombone in the Jefferson High School band under Sam Browne with a cohort that included Frank Morgan, Eric Dolphy, and Don Cherry. Jazz musicians such as Lionel Hampton would stop by to take him to rehearsal or to a club —Tapscott turned down Julliard, claiming he learned more at the "SWU" ("SideWalk University") of LA's jazz community. Rhythm and blues musicians came to his house, his family sung gospel at church, blues records resounded out of neighborhood windows, and his parents loved opera. His compositions contain all of these elements, and in addition, African rhythms, church choirs, and the spiritual jazz of Alice Coltrane.

Joel Dinerstein

QIJ - LA

Created by Joel Dinerstein · 13 songs, 1 hr 33 min

FOLLOWERS 0

PLAY (...)

Download

	TITLE	ARTIST	ALBUM		
▷	Frenesi - 1998 Digital Remaster	Gerry Mulligan	The Original Quartet W...	2019-07-29	3:11
▷	Let's Get Lost	Chet Baker	My Ideal	2019-07-30	3:45
▷	It's All Right With Me	Art Farmer & Benny Go...	Meet The Jazztet	2019-08-05	3:56
▷	Soy Califa - 2005 Digital Remaster	Dexter Gordon	A Swingin' Affair	2019-09-02	6:28
▷	Work Song	Charles Mingus	Mingus At The Bohemia	2019-09-02	5:26
▷	Ysabel's Table Dance - 1957/62 Master Takes	Charles Mingus	Tijuana Moods	2020-04-23	10:29
▷	Blues In	Art Pepper	Modern Art	2019-08-03	6:01
▷	Round Midnight - Live at the Jazz Standard	Frank Morgan	City Nights (Live at the...	2020-04-23	6:20
▷	Also sprach Zarathustra	Deodato	CTI: The Master Collec...	2020-04-23	8:59
▷	Red Clay	Freddie Hubbard	Red Clay (CTI Records...	2020-04-23	12:10
▷	Desert Fairy Princess (Live)	Horace Tapscott with T...	Soul Jazz Records Pres...	2019-08-01	11:20
▷	Change of the Guard	Kamasi Washington	The Epic	2019-10-08	12:16

7. Dinerstein's Los Angeles City playlist.

Like Frank Morgan, Tapscott played Central Avenue clubs as a teenager and apprenticed in Gerald Wilson's Orchestra. Unlike Morgan, he avoided the "heroin cliques" of Dex and others. He served four years in the Air Force, then returned to play in Lionel Hampton's band, found some studio work, and played occasional club gigs. To signal his music's spiritual aspect, he founded the Union of God's Musicians and Artists Ascension (UGMAA) and "The Ark" played The Immanuel United Church of Christ on the last Sunday of every month for eight years.

Listen to "Desert Fairy Princess" (1979): here he extends a single melodic theme into a hypnotic modal composition indebted to "Caravan". The piano opens with a simple bassline, echoed by percussion, all the while laying down a foundation for the flute to play the melody —this is much like opera, where the flute represents the "fairy princess". The gravitas of the melody builds the experience of en-*trancement* through repetition with tension provided by a counter-riff on the tubas and trombones. There is an initial climax (@ 2:45) that fades into a quiet interlude of dense harmonies. The flute then calls the procession back and leads the Arkestra across the desert with only the drummer's shifting figures for company. After eight minutes, a tuba solo emerges as if the earth itself has been given voice. When the flute re-states the melody, these contrasting voices create an expansive aural experience. This hybrid of classical music, African rhythms, and improvisation can also be heard in "Village Dance", an awakening rendered over nearly a half-hour through layers of percussion that ground epic solos on violin, saxophone, flute, and piano, the voices of the community.

In contrast to the Arkestra, Tapscott's trio and quintet albums are meditative and spiked with dissonance. The 17-minute opening track of his first album, *The Giant is Awakened* (1969), has the feel of a passion play: a single chord, multiple rhythmic layers, and a prophesying saxophone voice (altoist Arthur Blythe) *"awaken"* an imaginary audience. His piano technique combines Monk's melodic imagination with McCoy Tyner's rhythmic lyricism and the banged-out tonal clusters of Cecil Taylor.

Tapscott's music signals the last flickering of the Central Avenue scene as he kept the community's spirit alive across three decades of drug scourges, police brutality, and incarceration after the Watts riots. Tapscott "was all about community building", the young saxophonist Kamasi Washington reflected, and mentoring from "a socially-conscious perspective". His Arkestra rarely went on tour: "Here was a group led by this world-renowned musician who left the doors open to anyone in the community who wanted to be a part of it", the young saxophonist added, "[and] that saved a lot of lives".

Kamasi Washington's Afro-Futurist Jazz World

Kamasi Washington's *The Epic* is a twenty-first century jazz manifesto —a three-hour 3-CD debut album that comes charging out of the gate proclaiming a new era with its twelve-minute opening track, "Change of the Guard". In the opening movement, a driving horn riff pushes against a hard, fast, bluesy piano solo over funky layers of dark rhythm and strings when suddenly a sci-fi gospel choir enters to dialogue with piano and trumpet solos —as if guiding jazz into the future evocatively through our sonic associations with pop-culture. As this chaotic mélange slowly dissipates, Washington enters for a three-minute solo that builds from rhythm-and-blues figures into the passionate, distorted musical squawks of free jazz: he is the lone fighting sax-man taking on *the whole damned world* —a sonic Kung Fu battle represented in sound. Just before the nine-minute mark, the melody is rejoined in mellower form: Washington falls back into the hornline, the drums push the strings until they toughen up, the sci-fi chorus settles into the mix. Ambient electronica takes over for the final ninety seconds in a fragmented duet with the piano.

Where did this jazz come from, with its 10-piece jazz band augmented by a 20-person choir and a 32-piece orchestra? This innovative mix drew on Washington's experience playing in church choirs, the arias in Igor Stravinsky's *Symphony of Psalms,* and the drums-and-chant of Max Roach's *Freedom Now Suite.* There were also a series of "prophetic dreams" during the recording process that led to Washington's jazz vision within a crucible of Black consciousness.

Washington grew up in South Central LA and his father, a jazz musician influenced by Coltrane and Pharoah Sanders, often took him to see Tapscott's Arkestra. His neighborhood was full of jazz's "social consciousness and there was a great sense of community" through bandleader Gerald Wilson and drummer Billy Higgins. "Where else in L.A. could you go where there were four jazz clubs, poetry, a blues club and people playing in the park, all in a two-block area?" Washington played with the Arkestra as a teenager; his first paid gig was in Gerald Wilson's saxophone section. "That whole dense scene —that is [my] sound", he claims, referring to the epic sweep and rhythmic layers of those large-scale musical units. The mystical aspect draws on Alice Coltrane's mix of jazz, gospel, and Eastern religion.

In addition, the jazz and hiphop scenes have long been intertwined in LA. Washington's first steady gig was in Snoop Dogg's band, who were all jazz musicians. Jazz groups had poets freestyling over their grooves; jazz musicians went to gospel jam sessions. Washington's jazz collaborative is called the West Coast Get Down and its rhythm section are childhood friends: bassist Miles Mosley, fusion guitarist Thundercat (Stephen Lee Bruner), and his brother, drummer Ronald Bruner Jr. DJ Flying Lotus (Steven Ellison) runs Washington's record label (Brainfeeder) and one of his major influences is Alice Coltrane, his great aunt.

The final factor in Washington's breakthrough was the vision of LA engineer and producer Daddy Kev. At Kev's legendary Wednesday night pop-up club, Low End Theory, DJs melded hiphop, jazz, and electronica. Thundercat and Flying Lotus built on the genres' shared elements there —fragmentation, improvisation, shifting grooves, rhythmic textures— to create innovative soundscapes. Washington started coming by the club in 2015, just as Thundercat was working on Kendrick Lamar's *To Pimp a Butterfly*, the album that launched this scene into national consciousness.

Washington's albums are akin to soundtracks for unmade Afrofuturist martial arts films. The opening track of his *Heaven and Earth* is "Fists of Fury", named for a Bruce Lee film about fighting against Western imperialism. The vocalist proclaims political defiance: "*Our time as victims is over / We will no longer ask for justice / Instead we will take our retribution*". Once called "the jazz voice of Black Lives Matter", Washington's Afrofuturism is beat-driven, evocatively cinematic, and engineered for aural immersion. The West Coast Get Down collective has taken the LA past —of tentets, Central Avenue, and The Ark— into the new millennium.

Los Angeles Jazzes TomorrowLand

"Central Avenue was the beginning of the bebop era but also the beginning of the rock era", Art Farmer recalled. Big Jay McNeely's iconic, honking saxophone solos came off *the Avenue*, as did rhythm-and-blues hits such as "The Honeydripper", "Deacon's Hop", and T-Bone Walker's "Stormy Monday". These songs were recorded for black-owned labels (e.g., Aladdin, Imperial) and often featured jazz musicians as session men. Even Charlie Parker wailed some blues solos on three-minute R&B records with vocals, such as "Romance Without Finance". As Jay McNeely once said, "they never knew I started off playing jazz".

From Bebop to Rock on Central Avenue

One 1968 album marks a meeting ground of LA jazz, Hollywood *noir* themes, African-American resistance to racism, and Tapscott's community music: *Sonny's Dream – Birth of the New Cool* by altoist Sonny Criss, the kid transformed by Bird's first visit to LA. Tapscott composed and arranged this set of six originals, conducted the tentet, and created a sound that bears the scars of the Watts riot. Criss's alto surfs again and again into the tentet's blend of hard bop, big band, and R&B, a sonic battle with cinematic resonance. "Sonny's Dream" rushes out like a train then quickly resolves into a catchy *noir*-ish theme. Criss's solos are searing statements of survival ("The Black Apostles") while the piano solos moderate his intensity. Central Avenue saxophonist Teddy Edwards brings some ironic blues laughter to his solos, a counterpart to Criss's cries, while Tapscott's dark, bottom-heavy brass arrangements of tuba, bass, trombone, and baritone sax mark the community's sorrows.

By 1960, most LA musicians had left town and become integrated into the New York scene. Gerry Mulligan brought his baritone sax to an illuminating California-meets-New-York duet album, *Monk and Mulligan*. Mingus was New York's most important composer and bandleader between Monk and Coltrane. Art Farmer often won the *Downbeat* poll for best trumpeter —and recorded the brilliant *Modern Art*— but never received the accolades of Chet Baker. Yet his sixty-plus albums are of a consistently high caliber and his was an exemplary career in what jazz musicians simply call "the life".

LA's jazz scene was one path through which *jazz-as-art* morphed into *jazz-as-popular-culture*. Jazz arrangers composed many themes of *noir*-style detective shows (e.g., *Mission Impossible*), sitcoms (e.g., *M*A*S*H*), and cartoons. The sly, slinky riff of *The Pink Panther* (1963) was played by LA saxophonist

Plas Johnson; Charlie Parker often inserted the *Woody Woodpecker* theme into his solos. The popular crime drama *Peter Gunn* deserves special note: the detective had his home base at a jazz club and its theme was a top-ten hit, later recorded by everyone from Sarah Vaughn to Jimi Hendrix. A knock-off show, *Johnny Staccato, Jazz Detective,* featured indie filmmaker John Cassavetes as a jazz pianist-sleuth.

Three icons of the LA scene's musicians had momentous comebacks in the New York of the 1980s —Art Pepper, Frank Morgan, and Dexter Gordon— and each influenced a return to acoustic jazz and away from fusion. Make it four, if we count the artful *noir*-ish documentary of Chet Baker —*Let's Get Lost (1988)*— released the year of his passing.

Jazz started in New Orleans as a popular music combining ragtime, folk musics, Afro-Caribbean rhythms, classical and popular musics. A century later, jazz remains a crucible of new musical fusions of hiphop, rock, funk, electronica, Latin rhythms, and spiritual jazz. Flying Lotus's *You're Dead!* (2014) was acclaimed upon release as an Afrofuturist electronic hiphop jazz fusion concept album: Kamasi Washington's tenor murmurs in tandem with Thundercat's bass and jazz legend Herbie Hancock contributes keyboards; Kendrick Lamar surges through an electronic soundscape and Snoop Dogg raps back to fragmented video-game samples on "Dead Man's Tetris". This is just one variant of jazz's future streaming right now out of LA.

Chapter 6

QIJ - Jazz Beauty

Jazz Beauty is a ballad-heavy playlist that casts a wide net, from the virtuosic dialogue of jazz legends to a saxophone quartet's choir soundings. These tracks are musical diamonds that sparkle from a seamless integration of melodic and harmonic interplay, solos and ensemble sound, sonic textures and rhythmic layers. Consider these performances as the front room of an idiosyncratic jazz museum. For many listeners they will require no introduction.

Half these compositions begin with a compelling melody but others have a raw, rougher beauty that may seem abrasive at first, whether in the soloist's cry, an atonal trumpet solo, or blistering rhythms.

Yet repeated attention will, I hope, result in peeling past the listener's initial resistance to reveal depths of soulful self-expression and collective force.

To my ears, each track takes shape as a short story in musical form and here I offer a few sentences as to how each lives in my imagination.

Cannonball Adderley with Bill Evans, **"Waltz for Debby"**

> This is a lyrical meeting of musical minds, Evans' evanescent impressionism as peppered by Adderley's joyous swinging. It seems like a solo piano piece for a full minute until Adderley swings in like a lover who got off early from work. With his rich, warm tone, Adderley exemplifies how a jazz musician vocalizes his instrument with speech-like phrases, thoughtful pauses, staccato stops, grace-note hesitations, and exclamations of delight.

Billy Bang, *Waltz of the Water Puppets*

> Violinist Billy Bang's lush composition overlays a modal structure onto a Vietnamese folk melody to create musical healing. Each time the pentatonic melody is repeated, there is deeper en-*trance*-ment. Each successive solo —on flute, violin,

piano— emerges organically then dissolves back into the ensemble, including one on the *dan tranh,* a Vietnamese 16-string zither.

Mulatu Astatke & The Heliocentrics, *Phantom of the Panther*

The creator of Ethiopian jazz here crosses a seeming shaman's spell with the foreboding of a horror film soundtrack. Crystalline wind chimes sprinkle magic dust on an aggressive bassline, as if we have entered a haunted house. Halfway through, a harp enters and its ethereal sound dispels the gloom yet only deepens the short piece's psychedelia.

Sonny Rollins, *A Nightingale Sang in Berkeley Square*

After some early-morning piano, Sonny Rollins rises like the sun. His sonic power sheds light onto this standard as if blowing open the gate of a small city park to awaken the ears, minds, and spirits of its dogwalkers. Then he stops to ruminate after a minute, as if on the events of the previous evening. The piano then takes over with a set of rolling chords, a reminder of the day's demands. Time to hit the day, awakened.

Joel Dinerstein

QIJ – Jazz Beauty

Created by Joe Dinerstein • 12 songs, 1 hr 8 min

FOLLOWERS 0

PLAY

Download

TITLE	ARTIST	ALBUM		
Waltz For Debby	Cannonball Adderley, Bill E.	Know What I Mean? [Origi...	2019-04-10	5:18
Goodbye Pork Pie Hat	Charles Mingus	Mingus Ah Um	2019-04-29	4:48
Folk Song	Jan Garbarek	Folk Songs	2019-01-17	8:12
Caravan	Oscar Peterson, Dizzy Gille...	Oscar Peterson & Dizzy Gill...	2019-06-20	6:58
Phantom Of The Panther	Mulatu Astatke, The Helioc...	Inspiration Information 3	2019-03-10	2:21
Waltz of The Water Puppets	Billy Bang	Vietnam: Reflections	2019-04-02	6:48
Conference Of The Birds	Dave Holland Quartet	Conference Of The Birds	2019-02-13	4:39
Ming	David Murray	Ming	2019-04-10	4:28
Lonely Woman	Ornette Coleman	The Shape Of Jazz To Come	2019-03-09	5:02
The Peacocks	Stan Getz, Jimmy Rowles	The Peacocks	2019-02-13	5:40
Come Sunday	World Saxophone Quartet	Plays Duke Ellington	2019-02-27	7:33
Redemption Song	Harriet Tubman	The Terror End Of Beauty	2020-01-13	6:13

8. Dinerstein's Jazz Beauty playlist.

Oscar Peterson and Dizzy Gillespie, *Caravan*

Two veteran jazz masters play a wondrous duet. Peterson spreads the keyboard as if warming up, then plays the familiar Ellington melody, ending with a cascading run that Gillespie echoes in his first descending line. The trumpeter withdraws then dive-bombs from the upper register and, in the duet's first transcendent moment, Peterson sneaks in a buoyant bassline that instantly meshes with Dizzy's line (@ 00:34). This bassline recurs every minute during the duo's ongoing magical convergences.

World Saxophone Quartet (WSQ), *Come Sunday*

The WSQ transform into an avant-garde gospel choir that conveys reverence and solemnity in Duke Ellington's sonic portrait of African-American church-going. At times the quartet seems to breathe together, creating rich harmonies that break off into wild solo flights of ecstatic prayer. There are four parts: two minutes of quartet harmonizing; ninety seconds in which the quartet splits into two arguing pairs; a long three-minute solo; and the final resolution. The centerpiece is David Murray's tenor solo, a man wrestling with all his angels and devils. He scales upwards to the tenor's highest range as if in supplication —writhing, grieving, stomping, testifying— while being held down by supporting riffs. When the trio of saxes drops out, he is left alone in musical space: he roars and squeals, a last purge of the past week's regrets. Then the quartet unites —as if with raised horns— in a final gesture of praise.

Charlie Haden + Jan Garbarek + Egberto Gismonti, *Folk Song* (1981)

This composition sounds like the origin story of an indigenous people as retold at an annual festival. The interplay of this unusual global trio of guitar, sax, and bass shows jazz's cross-cultural reach. This meditation is alternately cerebral and spiritual, rhythmically hypnotic without a drum: Brazilian guitarist Egberto Gismonti fingerpicks grounding patterns for Norwegian saxophonist Jan Garbarek's raga-like lines while bassist Charlie Haden thrums resounding open, low tones. The saxophone calls the mind to communion in the first third; the guitar plays one's heart-strings in the second; the bass resonates like the earth speaking in the last.

Jimmy Rowles and Stan Getz, *The Peacocks*

A haunting midnight melody calls two sensitive souls into subdued conversation. Built of simple, recurring thematic ideas, piano and tenor improvise while a lavender sky bleeds into morning. The main saxophone riff descends and feathers each time, as if trying to break free, unsuccessfully, of melancholy.

Dave Holland Quartet, *Conference of the Birds*

This composition seems plucked out of the air, as if we are overhearing a conversation of philosophical birdmen. The opening minute-long bass solo sounds like an offering. Musical rattling snakes herald the arrival of the beautiful melody, played on flute and clarinet, steadied only by light fingertips on the bass. The flute and clarinet soar like musical kites weaving ephemeral patterns of enchantment in the sky.

Ornette Coleman, **Lonely Woman**

This was an original kind of blues wailing in 1960, a fragile melody with tensile strength —sweet and abrasive, yearning and assertive. The composition is symmetrical:

bass-and-drums open and close the piece while the horns ascend as if to console the lonely woman.

Charles Mingus, **Goodbye Pork Pie Hat** (1959)

Mingus composed this elegy for Lester Young upon hearing of the legendary tenor's passing in June 1959. It is a tonal portrait of a man known for his revolutionary modern tenor sound, humor, and endless flow of ideas. The sauntering pace of the ballad reflects Young's slow, unhurried stride coming down the block in his porkpie hat.

Harriet Tubman, **Redemption Song** (2018)

Jazz has expanded our aesthetic palette and this piece is thus a fitting end to the list, a searing track from a recent album, *The Terror End of Beauty.* There is a brutal beauty here in this compelling, harsh, reverberating, dissonant performance. It is hard to find Bob Marley's melody but the song's themes resound in the rumbling drone and roaring guitar. It sounds like three warrior musicians on a quest to create tougher spirits of its audience to fight for something better next time around.

Chapter 7

Playlist - The Groove

In sync, in phase, in the pocket —a groove is so much more than a beat. As Albert Murray wrote in *Stomping the Blues*, "African drummers had to serve a long period of rigidly supervised apprenticeship before being entrusted with such an awesome responsibility as carrying the beat!" Expansive, shifting, fluid, propulsive —the groove is the realm of the rhythm section. This is the deep cool of jazz, its profound beating heart.

The surface level may be intense, blistering, calm, atonal, cacophonous —yet underneath there is a rhythm section holding down the beat. At first, focus on the instruments producing each track's foundational groove. Once grounded, listen for the interplay of soloist and the rhythm section of piano-bass-drums.

MAST's re-envisioning of Thelonious Monk's classic **"Bemsha Swing"** (2018) has an infectious groove that instantly gets inside the listener's mind and body. MAST is the one-man studio-band of Tim Conley and melody and groove are inextricable here as the synth drives the solos into and out of this tune's expansive simplicity.

Bassist Esperanza Spalding's **"I Know You Know"** (2008) lassoes Brazilian rhythms into the jazz 4/4, mixing a samba feeling with funk and hinting at jazz's original syncopation through the New Orleans/Havana connection. Spalding's imaginative vocal lines in the higher register contrast with her controlled basslines while piano and congas help sound out a contemporary jazz/pop language.

Herbie Hancock's **"Watermelon Man"** (1962) is so ubiquitous it is probably playing somewhere in the world right now. The melody is the composer's vocalized memory of a fruit vendor from his Chicago youth, while its loping rhythm reflects the man's wagon wheels going over the cobblestones. The melody and horn riffs of this 16-bar blues are so rhythmically strong they seem to draw the solos of Freddie

Hubbard (trumpet) and Dexter Gordon (tenor) down into the groove.

The Cinematic Orchestra's "**Man With A Movie Camera**" (2002) reflects the convergence of jazz and electronica with its playful theme, sustained horn riffs, waves of synth, and creative drum programming. Written as a soundtrack to a silent film, the band's layering of sound suggests a film going through a projector.

Joni Mitchell's shift to jazz in the 1970s produced a rare, successful fusion of folk, rock, pop, and swing in songs such as "**In France They Kiss on Main Street**" (1975). Her band of LA studio musicians create a midrange groove anchored by electric bass and Fender Rhodes that meld perfectly with Mitchell's cooled alto voice.

The rock-ish groove of Charlie Hunter's "**No Money, No Honey**" (2016) gets smeared by drunken R&B horns and an ornery, soaring trumpet. The rhythm section holds it all together in a loose, funky pocket and Hunter's custom seven-string electric guitar enjoys some call-and-response with each horn.

TITLE	ARTIST	ALBUM		
			📅	Download ⏱
				FOLLOWERS 0
Bemsha Swing	MAST	Thelonious Sphere Monk	2019-04-12	3:44
I Know You Know	Esperanza Spalding	Esperanza	2019-12-07	3:45
Watermelon Man - Remastered 2007	Herbie Hancock	Takin' Off (Rudy Van Gelde	12 days ago	7:09
Man With The Movie Camera	The Cinematic Orchestra	Every Day	2019-11-26	9:10
In France They Kiss on Main Street	Joni Mitchell	The Hissing Of Summer La...	2019-11-17	3:20
No Money, No Honey	Charlie Hunter	Everybody Has A Plan Until...	2019-12-05	3:53
3 Wishes	Ornette Coleman, Jerry Ga...	Virgin Beauty	2019-04-26	4:19
Nuyorican Son	Bobby Sanabria	Luna Latina - The Best Of L...	9 days ago	5:22
Caravan (Remastered)	Duke Ellington	By Popular Demand Duke E...	2019-01-27	4:15
St. Thomas	Sonny Rollins, Tommy Flan...	Saxophone Colossus	2019-11-26	6:48
Rumble In The Jungle	Max Roach	M'Boom	2019-04-22	7:15
Wrap Your Troubles In Dreams - Live At The Villag...	Bill Evans	California, Here I Come	12 days ago	6:49

QIJ - Groove

Joel Dinerstein

Created by Joel Dinerstein · 12 songs, 1 hr 5 min

PLAY

9. Dinerstein's Groove playlist.

In "**3 Wishes**" (1988), Ornette Coleman and Jerry Garcia dance together happily and harmolodically in the North African desert. After ninety seconds of the alto's piercing pied piper call, Garcia's solo goes straight into the thick of the groove, moving in and out of the stacked sound, lightening it, settling in, traveling along. The Prime Time band maintains a funky set of electric lines throughout, continually entangling and disentangling the caravan's movement.

Drummer Bobby Sanabria's "**Nuyorican Son**" blasts the Latin sound of upper Manhattan back down Broadway, combining Cuban and Puerto Rican rhythms with Ellington's orchestral sound into a declaration of his "Nuyo-rican" identity. Latin jazz is a major story of twenty-first century jazz and Sanabria's *Big Band Urban Folktales* (2007) draws on its roots in 1940s New York.

"**Caravan**" (1936) has a groove so deep, wide, and universal, it has been covered by surf and salsa bands (Dick Dale, The Ventures, Tito Puente), country and rock guitarists (Chet Atkins, Duane Eddy), and even the Balkan Brass band. Duke Ellington and Juan Tizol composed the minor key melody and its North African groove creates a sense of steady, dynamic movement across a desert while Ellington shows his stride piano chops on his minute-long solo.

The Caribbean groove of Sonny Rollins's **"St. Thomas"** (1957) has been the classic jazz sound of *carnaval* for sixty years. When Rollins' big tenor sound drops out, the beat is simply carried by the crisp *tss-tss-tss* on the high-hat. Listen for how the piano solo carries the habanera beat, the "Spanish tinges" —from Spain, Cuba, and the Argentinian tango— that first infused jazz in New Orleans.

What would a drum circle of master drummers from the African diaspora sound like? One answer can be heard on **"Rumble in the Jungle"**, a hypnotic track from Max Roach's M'Boom (1980). Out of this percussion collective's steady, shifting rhythms emerge solos on tom-toms, marimba, tympani, vibes, and steel pan. This album illuminates the relationship between melody, rhythm, and percussion.

Bill Evans invented the interplay of the modern jazz piano trio —three instruments working as a mobile equilateral triangle rather than as soloist and back-up musicians. **"Wrap Your Troubles In Dreams"** (1967) is an uptempo standard, a joyous romp in which the piano keys ring off the cymbals while the hesitation in the melody produces an exhilarating anticipation.

Chapter 8

Playlist - The Ensemble

The focus here is on small-unit ensembles of five-to-seven pieces, bands that channeled the swing and power of big bands into a leaner, more flexible format. If big bands were trains, these ensembles were sleek sedans —Jaguars, BMWs— with power, style, and dynamic control on the curves. Key ensembles include those of Cannonball Adderley, Carla Bley, James Carter, and David Murray.

Jazz musicians are not beholden to a classical ideal of playing in unison but rather to the African principle of "apart-playing". Musicians play together but each has a separate voice —a voice *apart*— even when blended into other horns, as here on "Dat Dere" or "Stolen Moments". Some of these ensembles were working bands but some were one-offs that somehow sound just as *together*.

Pianist and songwriter Mose Allison leads an urbane pick-up band in "**Ever Since the World Ended**" (1987), his satire on apocalypse. Influenced by Ellington's swinging flow, Allison's bluesy piano complements the wry irony of his vocals. The two saxes comment like a Greek chorus, then halfway through, altoist Arthur Blythe's solo protests then adjusts to the new order.

Arthur Blythe's "**Down San Diego Way**" is a light, swinging Sunday afternoon jam from his classic *Lenox Avenue Breakdown* (1978). With its long flute solo and pumping tuba, its congas and Jack DeJohnette's drums, this ensemble just relaxes into this one-chord vamp as if they have all the time in the world. The group does not play the theme until three-quarters of the way through and we didn't even miss it.

James Carter's "**Layin' in the Cut**" is a turn-of-the-millennium groove with the saxophonist taking on each member of the unit one-by-one with funk then grit then power. When the band falls out, Carter first plays skronk lines then just seems to pluck the saxophone before fading into a beautiful ten-second hum. The groove is powered by Ornette Coleman's original harmolodic rhythm section.

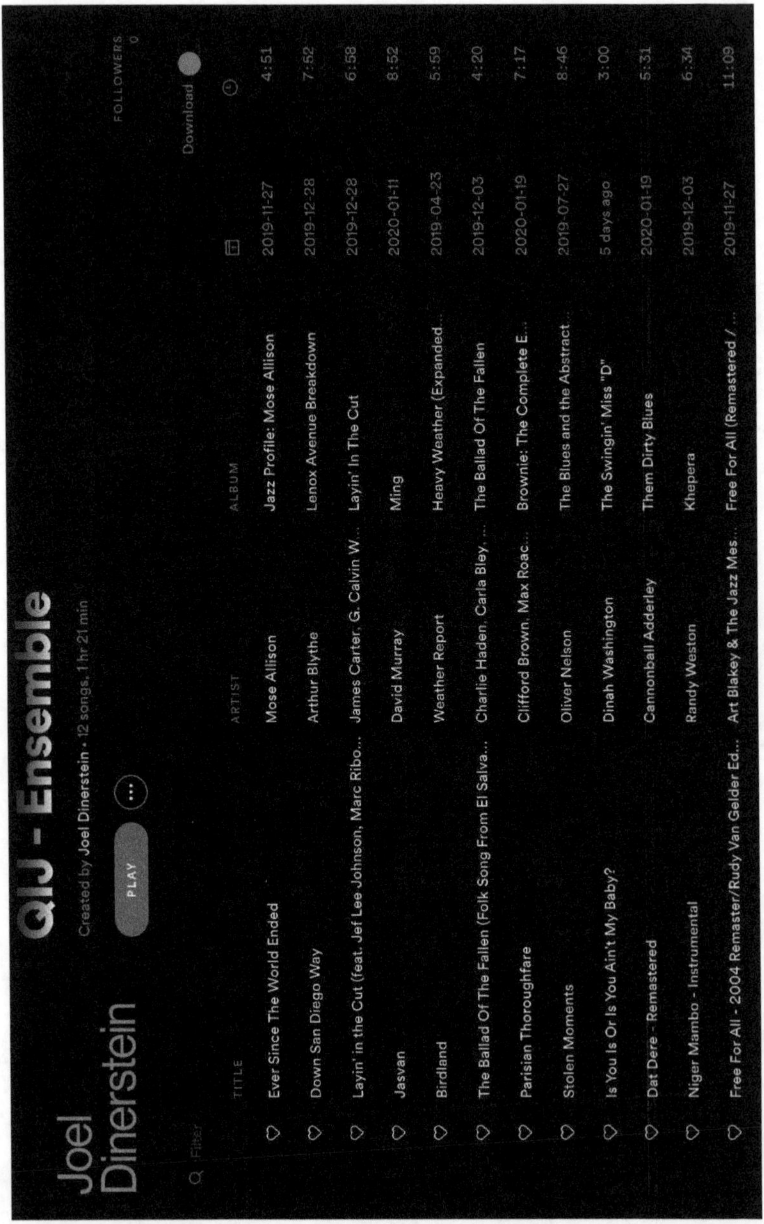

10. Dinestein's Ensemble playlist.

Beneath the pretty melody of the David Murray Octet's **"Jasvan"** (1981), this group creates such intricate polyphony they feel like subplots threatening to subvert the song's main line. Two instruments will take a motif and digress, the bassist argues with the saxophonist, the drummer and bassist split their attentions —it is a pleasantly bumpy ride of many roads simultaneously taken.

Weather Report's **"Birdland"** (1978) was a jazz hit and the first third builds to an exuberant big-band-style theme but played by a small fusion combo. Keyboardist Joe Zawinul wrote the song in tribute to the iconic New York jazz club named for Charlie Parker, where he first heard Armstrong, Basie, Ellington and Miles.

Carla Bley and Charlie Haden's Liberation Music Orchestra create a subtle kind of musical grandeur in **"Ballad of the Fallen" (1982),** with its Salvadoran folk melody, symphonic orchestration, and lilting dance groove. Expressive and emotive, the group raises this folk theme to nearly revolutionary consciousness.

Trumpeter Clifford Brown mimics car horns as Max Roach's cymbals ting to render the sound of Paris in the 1950s on **"Parisian Thoroughfare"** (1954). This composition also commemorates the city's community of postwar expatriate African-American jazz musicians.

Oliver Nelson's **"Stolen Moments"** (1961) has a beautiful melody and artful solos that create a cumulative impact as if of a jeweled mosaic of blue stones. The profound solos of trumpet, flute, and alto sax —by Freddie Hubbard, Eric Dolphy, and Oliver Nelson— dissolve into Bill Evans' concluding piano solo.

Dinah Washington and Quincy Jones were both unclassifiable musicians and their version of **"Is You Is Or Is You Ain't My Baby?"** connects swing, pop, and jazz with rhythm-and-blues. Washington first pitches the question sweetly and playfully, then it becomes softly urgent with the help of the walking bass, then she gets a bit worried along with that growling trombone. The arrangement is near-perfect with the flute, bass, and saxophone all playing key roles on this gem from the classic album, *The Swingin' Miss D* (1957).

Pianist Bobby Timmons' **"Dat Dere"** (1960) validates African-American vernacular speech in the title and with its gospel chords. The melody percolates through the solos by the Adderley brothers (Cannonball on alto, Nat on trumpet) then Timmons takes a bluesy solo full of block chords that swings it back home.

Pianist and composer Randy Weston has studied African music in depth and **"Niger Mambo"** comes from an album exploring ancient relationships between Africa and China *(Khepera*, 1998). Written with his long-time partner, the trombonist and arranger Melba Liston, this metaphorical mambo kicks off with a thunderous opening.

Art Blakey and the Messengers' **"Free For All"**, is a barnburner —a surging, propulsive eleven-minute track that never lets up. Composer Wayne Shorter's pun is actually a stirring political call to *freedom-for-all*. Blakey's drum leadership and raw percussive power is ubiquitous: during each spirited solo, the supporting horns sound a high-pitched battle-cry for freedom (@2:00). The song is a river of sound in which the rapids come fast and furious, with each solo wrangling with the currents.

Chapter 9
Playlist - The Blues

All African-American musical forms partake in an aesthetic of uplift: the audience is meant to be revitalized whether leaving the church, juke joint, nightclub, or dance floor. This objective is built into the musical culture's DNA —whether in jazz, blues, gospel, funk, soul, rock-and-roll, or hiphop. Even if blues conjures up the image of a solo guitarist moaning about mistreatment, the guitarist means to help an audience find some psychological ventilation from listening to his valid gripes. And there are happy blues, blues marches, and funky blues.

Blues is essential to jazz due to its basic framework, infinite possibilities, and ethnic rootedness. Its three-chord form allows improvising musicians to create a spontaneous emotional response or offer a tribute to a fallen musician: the statement may be one of joy or defiance, of depression or coded political protest.

Blues has two functions for jazz ensembles: (a) as a given *tone* or *feeling* for a composition or a solo; (b) as a tight, simple structure for improvising. This playlist runs the gamut from soulful sorrow to extravagant expression to symphonic richness. And don't miss the laughter within the horn solos.

"**Cool Blues**" (1947) is a classic 12-bar blues written by Charlie Parker and he swings deeply on its jaunty two-bar theme, enjoying the guidance of the walking bass. For jazz musicians, "I'm cool" meant *being relaxed in one's own style,* in control of the situation, *chill.* Parker models the concept here by alternating expressive phrases with musical space.

On the classic ***Blues and Roots*** (1959), Charles Mingus arranged and molded the folk materials of blues, gospel, and New Orleans music into complex compositions. "**Cryin' Blues**" starts with a familiar melancholy yet breaks into an upbeat second movement with innovative call-and-response. The soloist is challenged, consoled, and mocked by the horn section, like friends working to rock him out of his depression.

"Moanin'" is also from *Blues and Roots* and Pepper Adams's opening, swooping baritone sax riff becomes the song's thematic axis. By the ninety-second mark, Mingus is cheering on the ensemble like a coach: the horns split into multiple lines *(polyphony)*, the rhythm section pumps a constant flow of energy, Mingus's bass bullies the soloists (@ 4:40). Then the trombones and saxophones battle each other into near-cacophony, a Mingus signature once called "chaos-is-breaking-out-all-over-our-heads". Mingus resolves the chaos twice with a swinging bridge so unexpectedly harmonious, it sounds like redemption itself (@1:46, 7:33).

James Carter's "**Deep Throat Blues**" is a 12-bar blues that puns on sex and saxophones with swaggering hornlines at-once playful, raunchy, and exploratory. Carter's riverine slurrings of notes are full of deep honks, macho strutting, and downward slides, but Dave Holland's bass always bounces our ears back into the fray. Few musicians make blues or virtuosity this much fun.

The Miles Davis Quintet's "**All Blues**" (1959) is an example of just how creative jazz musicians can be within the 12-bar blues format. This unusual time signature

(6/8) fits inside your mind like a waltz (1-2-3, 1-2-3). The intro rolls in like a spring mist on muted trumpet, the drummer's brushwork, and the piano's tremolo effect. Miles plays open trumpet for four choruses, followed by four choruses apiece by Adderley and Coltrane. The rhythm section generates impressive equilibrium, in part due to the piano's short connecting breaks after each solo. When Evans takes the last solo, it is as if we've been waiting for the piano to speak.

In "**Blue Monk / Stormy Monday**" (1987), the Dirty Dozen Brass Band runs jazz's blues foundation through the filter of New Orleans street-parade music. The band delivers Monk's theme with humor and verve until the trombone solo breaks off, following the bassline of sousaphonist Kirk Joseph. The seamless transition into "Stormy Monday" happens at the five-minute mark with the vocalist shouting his frustration. The band then shifts into a brassy shuffle until a growled trombone solo leads the band back into "Blue Monk".

Dave Douglas' "**Blues to Steve Lacy**" (2006) is a blues in feeling, tone, and mood rather than structure. This tribute honors the revered soprano saxophonist, a partner with Sonny Rollins on the Williamsburg Bridge and the first musician to understand Monk's genius. The interplay of trumpet and tenor echoes the LA sound of Baker/Mulligan until the electric piano adds a light layer of funk.

Mary Lou Williams shows off her piano chops on **"Bag's Blues"** —from an aptly-titled live album, *A Grand Night For Swinging* (1976)— by distilling the Kansas City style through just a piano trio.

Guitarist Bill Frisell fries up the opening riff of **"Come Together"** (2011) on an album of Beatles songs. Frisell has created a unique blend of country jazz by adding funk, guitar effects, and string instruments (violin and pedal steel) to his sound.

In **"Blues, Too"** (2015), the two crisp guitars of Nels Cline and Julian Lage fill a blank aural canvas with flatted blue notes, succinct phrasing, edgy runs, and refreshing pauses. After some spiky explorations, the duo finds a refreshing groove and blow dandelion notes into the wind. They then begin strumming together, regularly and repetitively, until producing the sound of a train (4:55) —then they ride it together to the end of the line.

Joel Dinerstein

Created by Joel Dinerstein · 13 songs, 1 hr 29 min

PLAY ⋯

🔍 Filter

FOLLOWERS

Download ⊕

	TITLE	ARTIST	ALBUM	📅	
▷	Cool Blues	Charlie Parker	Stupendous	2019-12-05	3:06
▷	Cryin' Blues	Charles Mingus	Blues & Roots	2019-11-30	5:03
▷	Moanin'	Charles Mingus	Blues & Roots	2019-12-05	8:03
▷	Deep Throat Blues	James Carter	The Real Quietstorm	2020-01-03	6:08
▷	All Blues	Miles Davis	Kind Of Blue	2019-06-10	11:33
▷	Blue Monk / Stormy Monday - Live	The Dirty Dozen Brass Band	Live: Mardi Gras In Montreux	2020-01-20	8:59
▷	Blues to Steve Lacy	Dave Douglas Quintet	Meaning and Mystery (feat....	2019-11-26	5:55
▷	Blue Train - Remastered	John Coltrane	Blue Train	2019-12-03	10:43
▷	Bag's Blues - Recorded Live in 1976	Mary Lou Williams	A Grand Night for Swinging ...	10 days ago	6:29
▷	Come Together	Bill Frisell	All We Are Saying... (Exclusi...	2019-10-02	5:10
▷	Blues, Too	Nels Cline, Julian Lage	ROOM	2019-12-05	7:01
▷	I Got The Blues In Santa Cruz	Horace Silver	The Hardbop Grandpop	2019-11-30	8:07
▷	Rocks In My Bed - 1999 Remastered	Duke Ellington	Never No Lament: The Blant...	5 days ago	3:07

11. Dinestein's Blues playlist.

John Coltrane's classic **"Blue Train"** (1958) transforms a 12-bar blues into an epic journey called to order by three horns playing its anthemic theme in unison. Staccato horn bursts prod Coltrane during his three-minute solo and create productive discord. Trumpeter Lee Morgan builds his own fire for two minutes then gives way to trombonist Curtis Fuller's majestic solo. Their three distinct voices reveal disparate personalities and approaches, generating the cumulative power of a spiritual journey.

Pianist and composer Horace Silver mocks his elder status on an album entitled *The Hardbop Grandpop* with "**I Got The Blues in Santa Cruz**" (1996). Nobody gets the blues in this California beach town —that's the joke— as illustrated by the song's chill vibe. The opening bassline pours out a warm theme: the trumpet offers a piercing solo and the tenor a gritty one, yet neither dents the drummer's easy, fluid swinging. Then Silver enters with rolling octaves, leads a call-and-response with the horns, and then, well, it's probably just back to the bar.

Duke Ellington wrote **"Rocks in My Bed"** (1941) for vocalist Ivie Anderson and the orchestral moodiness masks this 12-bar blues until she enters seductively and tells her tale of unwanted solitude. Although no longer famous, Anderson owned and ran a major jazz venue on LA's Central Avenue, Ivie's Chicken Shack.

Chapter 10

Playlist - Sound and Solo

A musician's sound is profoundly individual. It is, in effect, the projection of one's personality —a singular aesthetic revealed through musical ideas and stylistic tropes. As Charlie Parker once said, "Music is your own experience, your own thoughts, your wisdom. If you don't live it, it won't come out of your horn".

Miles Davis put it this way: "The underlying task, the core of the task [in jazz], is sound. Sound is your very own voice. Sound is in charge of your person. You are your own sound". A jazz musician's sound reflects his or her felt, lived experience. "I write to each man's sound", Duke Ellington often said, "a man's sound is his total personality". Vocalist Betty Carter summed up this core challenge: "Everybody wants a sound".

A musician's sound means all of the following: tone, aesthetics, phrasing, vocalized inflections, preferred harmonies. "Everyone has a sound, just like everyone has a recognizable voice. Someone calls you on the phone, you answer and you know who it is by the voice", Charles McPherson said during a blindfold test about his fellow altoist, Lee Konitz. "It's his saxophone voice, and that's the way he is as a person —quiet, doesn't talk much, doesn't talk loud".

The expression of a musician's sound can best be heard in a solo, a personal statement within the structure of a song. In the jazz conversation, the soloist has the floor (so to speak).

Here I present six pairs of musicians to illuminate contrasting approaches to individual instruments: piano, bass, trumpet, alto saxophone, guitar, and vocals.

> Keith Jarrett, "**Part IV, Koln**" (1975). Jarrett is arguably the most renowned global jazz musician of the last half-century and this solo piano finale is an inspired spontaneous composition of beauty with structural integrity.

> Jason Moran, "**Gangsterism Over 10 Years**" (2010). Moran's style is more percussive than Jarrett's and his tonal clusters fit the more drum-centered trio he leads. His lyricism swings and he surprises the listener with tempo shifts and a crisp, ongoing dialogue with his drummer (Nasheet Waits).

Joel Dinerstein

Created by Joel Dinerstein · 13 songs, 58 min

PLAY

FOLLOWERS 0

Download

TITLE	ARTIST	ALBUM		
Köln, January 24, 1975, Pt. II C – Live	Keith Jarrett	The Köln Concert	2019-08-20	6:57
Gangsterism Over 10 Years	Jason Moran	TEN	10 days ago	6:56
I Can't Help It	Esperanza Spalding, Joe Lo...	Radio Music Society	10 days ago	4:42
Donna Lee	Jaco Pastorius	Jaco Pastorius	9 days ago	2:27
In The Still Of The Night	Lester Bowie	The Odyssey of Funk & Pop...	3 days ago	4:44
The Eraser	Christian Scott aTunde Adjuah	Yesterday You Said Tomorrow	10 days ago	5:26
Samba Cantina	Paul Desmond	Bossa Antigua	3 days ago	5:42
Far Cry	Eric Dolphy, Booker Little	Far Cry	a few secon...	3:53
American Garage	Pat Metheny Group	American Garage	2019-07-27	4:11
Sweet Georgia Brown	Django Reinhardt, Stéphane...	In Person	3 days ago	3:07
They Say It's Spring	Blossom Dearie	Verve Jazz Masters 51: Bloss...	10 days ago	3:40
Round Midnight	Betty Carter	Round Midnight + out There...	2019-07-27	3:20
Someone To Watch Over Me	Ella Fitzgerald	The Complete Decca Single...	9 days ago	3:16

12. Dinerstein's sound & solo playlist.

With "**Donna Lee**" (1976), bassist Jaco Pastorius kicked off his first album with Charlie Parker's fast bebop standard, an audacious choice. Solo bass albums were rare but so were Jaco's innovations: burbling electric basslines, harmonics, the groovy slide with which he caps off phrases. Two-and-a-half minutes and the jazz bassist's role was changed forever.

Esperanza Spalding, "**I Can't Help It**" (2012). This version of a Stevie Wonder tune is less a jazzy take on pop-music than a sophisticated regrooving of African-American musical forms. Spalding draws on four generations of rhythm-and-blues basslines while her voice enshrouds the listener. The tagline may give it a pop feel ("I can't *help* it") but how the vocal and bassline wind around each other, while sinking into the funk groove, is all jazz mastery.

In Lester Bowie's **"In the Still of the Night"** (1998), the trumpeter mixes mastery and playfulness on this doo-wop classic to create a performance that is *at-once* virtuosic, cartoonish, and braggadocious. Bowie starts with a burnished, regal tone, opens to a more emotive rhythm-and-blues call, swings the band, then deconstructs the song on his solo until he is just popping sonic syllables. There are four movements here: a thematic statement of yearning, ripening romantic hopes, solo confession with brass solidarity, and joyful restatement of communion.

In Christian Scott aTunde Adjuah's "**The Eraser**" (2010), his trumpet sounds like an advancing weather system with misty ragged edges and cool undercurrents. The opposite of Bowie's exuberance, Adjuah's muted trumpet harkens back to early Miles Davis, but this composition by Radiohead's Thom Yorke evokes a more futuristic soundscape. Born and raised in New Orleans, Adjuah has been performing live since he was 15 as the protégé of his uncle, the altoist Donald Harrison.

Paul Desmond, "**Samba Cantina**" (1964). Bossa nova is a perfect fit for Desmond's lilting alto sound with its flowing lines, melodic creativity, and cerebral swinging. Desmond was the altoist and co-composer in pianist Dave Brubeck's quartet for twenty-five years and composed the ubiquitous "Take Five". His complement here is guitarist Jim Hall, who lets his chords ring rather than strum, creating an open, uncluttered sound.

Eric Dolphy's **"Far Cry"** (1962) is a far cry indeed from Desmond. Dolphy's alto solos often leap upward then dive or lope along, a glider riding thermals and leaving behind luminescent skywriting. His thinner, more angular, wavering tone is full of innovative, graffitied sonic smears; as partnered here with trumpeter Booker Little, the two sound like Bird and Diz inflected by hard bop. An original musical thinker, Dolphy influenced both Mingus and Coltrane while in their bands.

Pat Metheny's "**American Garage**" (1979) was a jazz hit and sounds like a quartet's version of a hit rock single. Metheny's guitar sounds more like a light-saber made from molten steel than a lead rock guitarist's fuzzbombs yet at the three-minute mark, this song hits a solid 4/4 Chuck Berry groove and nearly bursts into Dionysian rock-and-roll.

Django Reinhardt's gypsy guitar swing was the first jazz to develop outside the US and on the early standard, "**Sweet Georgia Brown**" (1931), he carries the song with surefooted, buoyant strumming. Django's single-string solos provide bursts of open sky that dovetail beautifully with his long-time partner, violinist Stéphane Grappelli.

Blossom Dearie, **"They Say It's Spring" (1957).** Dearie's voice is an artistic confection that bedevils listeners with the paradox of girlish audacity. She sounds like a cross between Dorothy Parker and Audrey Hepburn, a knowing coquette in control of her flirtations and negotiations, an attitude summed up by her song, "Give Him the Ooh-La-La". Here she takes her sly, idiosyncratic time to tell the story of a new love that survives its spring fling.

Betty Carter, **"'Round Midnight"** (1963). Carter's virtuosic scatting, unusual phrasing, shifting tempos, and verbal skeins of blue notes turn every word of this Monk classic into a stone on an aural path. Her improvisational skills defy all vocal conventions: words shatter then glitter like diamonds as Carter carves new vocal trails with and through the horns.

Ella Fitzgerald, **"Someone to Watch Over Me"** (1951). Along with Sinatra, Ella carried the banner of the swing era —when jazz was popular music— for a half-century. Her voice is light and flowing, her interpretations lived, literal and reverent. In the 1950s, she sang nearly all of the American Songbook, composer by composer.

Jazz in the World,
The World in Jazz

Call 1917-2017 the jazz century. Jazz was global popular music from 1917-1945: it was the popular dance music of the Jazz Age, Swing Era, and World War II; it signified freedom in Europe during the Great Depression, wartime, and the Cold War. The core jazz practices of solos, improvisation, and rhythmic vitality threatened totalitarian governments: Nazi Germany banned jazz as "Judeo-Negroid music"; the Soviet Union suppressed jazz as the decadent music of capitalism. Yet even Nazi youth loved jazz and its swing dances while jazz historian S. Frederick Starr equated Communism and jazz as "The Two Revolutions of 1917". The Bolshevik Revolution failed in 1989; the jazz revolution is ongoing.

Jazz is more global than ever and its contemporary masters include the following: pianists Guillermo Klein (Argentina) and Hiromi Uehra (Japan); saxophonists Shabaka Hutchings (Barbadian-Black British) and Miguel Zenon (US/Puerto Rico); drummers Omar Sosa (Cuba) and Manu Katche (France); guitarists Lionel Loueke (Benin) and Lage Lund (Norway); vocalists Roberta Gambarini (Italy) and Eliane Elias (Brazil); bassists Linda Oh (Chinese-Malaysian-Australian) and Avishai Cohen (Israel). On an American scene once dominated by men, women constantly break new ground as composers, bandleaders, and groove-makers: key figures include bassist Esperanza Spalding, drummer Terri Lyne Carrington, guitarist Mary Halvorson, composer/ bandleader Maria Schneider, and vocalist Cassandra Wilson.

The jazz revolution transformed musical self-expression around the world, from Afro-Cuban music to Django Reinhardt's gypsy jazz, from Brazil's bossa nova to the Ethiopian jazz of Mulatu Astatke. The jazz revolution transformed global musical individuality, cultural politics, and dance floors; its practices have influenced nearly all musical genres, from rock to classical, from funk to hiphop to Afropop.

Consider the wedding of jazz and bossa nova in the early 1960s around Antonio Carlo Jobim's music. Tenor saxophonist Stan Getz produced two classic albums —*Getz/Gilberto* with Brazilian guitarist Joao Gilberto and *Jazz Samba* with American guitarist

Charlie Byrd— but Cannonball Adderley, Frank Sinatra, and Ike Quebec (among others) also made compelling albums in the subgenre.

Or consider this anecdote about one early marriage of African-American jazz and Cuban music through a chance meeting of pianist Herbie Hancock and percussionist Mongo Santamaria. Hancock and trumpeter Donald Byrd went to see Santamaria's Afro-Cuban band in the mid-1960s and when Byrd asked the bandleader to play a Latin jazz tune, he could not name one. Byrd suddenly asked Hancock to play this new song, "Watermelon Man", and the pianist went up and played the theme. Santamaria yelled, "Keep playing it!", leaped on stage and transmuted its underlying *habanera beat* to congas. The bassist then picked a bassline off Hancock's chords and the audience quickly hit the dance floor unsolicited. "This is a hit! This is fantastic!" Santamaria cried and he recorded its definitive version.

Then there are the jazz ambassadors of the 1950s chosen to show that the US was not a racist society: Benny Goodman, Louis Armstrong, and Dizzy Gillespie. Footage reveals that Armstrong was welcomed in Ghana as a returning prince of Africa. Gillespie refused to parrot the party line nor attend formal parties of the State Department; instead, he sought out local musicians, jammed on the streets, and spoke out about both colonialism and racism. "Night in Tunisia" was a particular favorite since its hybrid groove of Africa, Latin America, and American jazz left room for all manner of musicians to find an entry point.

QIJ - Postscript

Joel Dinerstein

Created by Joel Dinerstein · 13 songs · 1 hr 6 min

PAUSE

FOLLOWERS 0

Download

#	TITLE	ARTIST	ALBUM		
	Hola	Miguel Zenón	Sonero: The Music of Is...	2020-04-25	4:41
	Blackbird	Hiromi	Spectrum	2020-04-26	5:21
	Criss Cross	Avishai Cohen	Duende	2020-04-29	3:47
	Gaia	Lionel Loueke	GAIA	2020-04-29	3:46
	Go To Mexico	Cassandra Wilson	Thunderbird	2020-04-25	4:15
	Overlooking	Manu Katché, Patrick	The Scope	2020-04-25	3:35
	Superfly	Jazz Soul Seven, Terri L...	Impressions of Curtis...	2020-04-26	8:25
	My Mind I Find in Time	Mary Halvorson	Code Girl	2020-04-25	6:43
	You Don't What Love Is	Eliane Elias	I Thought About You (A...	2020-04-25	5:13
	Some Circles (Evanescence Version)	Maria Schneider	The Essential Maria Sc...	2020-04-25	5:52
	Watermelon Man	Mongo Santamaria	Mongo Santamaria's Gr...	2020-04-25	3:14
	Desafinado	Stan Getz, João Gilbert...	Getz / Gilberto	2020-04-25	4:16

13. Dinerstein's postscript playlist.

Jazz remains a generative source of artistic individuality, rhythmic power, sonic innovation, and musical textures. As early as 1924, conductor Leopold Stokowski gave notice to the planetary path jazz musicians might carve out: "Jazz is an expression of the times, of the breathless, energetic, superactive times in which we are living. The jazz players make their instruments do entirely new things, things finished [classical] musicians are taught to avoid. They are pathfinders into new realms".

The artistic challenges of jazz —to create a signature voice and style *in-the-moment*— emerged from the limitations on African-Americans. Their non-verbal declarations of freedom liberated musical instruments from tradition and instigated a validation of ethnic imaginations.

Jazz is the sonic document of an individual's human experience in conversation with others. Asked to define his objective for a recent album, saxophonist J.D. Allen said simply, "I want to just say I existed, man. I was here. This is a 'JD was here' on the wall".

The soloist symbolizes each of us living daily, trying to survive in style while carrying our personal burdens. When Miles Davis blasts his trumpet to carve a path into the funky chaos of *Bitches Brew* or Carla Bley conducts a free-jazz ensemble through the blues, each creates a musical tsunami only to fight it to a draw or, even better, surf it back to the shore supported by the band. The waves will always keep coming: the need to fight or ride remains.

Call it sonic existentialism, a key hidden musical philosophy of the twentieth century. Those who have ears to hear, let them listen. *And the beat goes on.*

Glossary

American cultural terms

Minstrelsy	This theatrical form of the mid-1800s featured music, comedy, and dance routines performed by white men who painted their faces black to mock the intelligence and culture of African-Americans. Now usually referred to as "blackface minstrelsy," the best performers later were African-Americans, who added the cakewalk dance that were globally influential.
Jitney	Jitneys were transportation services in the form of vans or small buses that followed a certain route but could be diverted to drop off or pick up passengers.
Jim Crow	The "Jim Crow era" was the common name for a set of laws that governed the strict segregation of whites and blacks between 1896-1954 in all public spaces, from theaters to trains to schools. The Supreme Court decision made "separate but equal" facilities legal in 1896.
"Scrapple from the Apple"	"The Apple" is a slang phrase for New York City and "a scrap" is slang for fighting. This Charlie Parker composition creates a pun and rhyme around musicians battling to create a joyful, artistic noise (a "scrapple") in New York City.
White society band	White society bands were dance orchestras that entertained upper-class white audiences, usually in hotels or elite ballrooms. These bands played soft, inoffensive music and often imitated African-American ragtime or jazz bands.

Second lines	Second lines are traditional weekly parades through New Orleans neighborhoods sponsored by a local club and organized around a marching brass band. The "second line" refers to the community of dancers while the "first line" consists of the club and the band.
Jazz funeral	Jazz funerals are New Orleans ritual processions that honor dead musicians and public figures with a parade to the cemetery. A dirge is played on the way to the burial and an uptempo hymn upon return.
Share cropping	Share cropping is a form of subsistence tenant farming that often kept families tied down to the whims of a wealthy landowner.
Underground railroad	The underground railroad was a network of secret routes used by slaves in the US South to escape to free Northern states and Canada. The phrase became a metaphor for "the road to freedom" and its "stations" were houses owned by white allies.
Rent party	A social event common in African-American communities in the 1920s where the host provided music and food in exchange for a donation to help pay rent on an apartment.
Cutting contest	A cutting contest was an exciting battle between jazz musicians of equal ability and an essential element of jazz's popularity from 1920-1960.

Specific musical terms

Businessman's bounce	The "businessman's bounce" was a 1920s slang term for a diluted form of uptempo New Orleans jazz. It referred to songs with just enough innovative rhythm (or syncopation) to lift the mood of businessmen either at lunch or at meetings with clients. It was often used as an insult by musicians to refer to upper-class audiences.
Down home blues	This is an African-American term for a danceable blues song in a traditional Southern United States groove, like from the Mississippi Delta.
Crack band	A "crack band" is a term of praise that refers to a reliable ensemble of professional musicians who have developed a chemistry from playing together.
Funk	Funk is a style of music that combines elements of rhythm-and-blues and soul, characterized by a percussive vocal style, stable harmonies, and a strong bass line with intense downbeats.
Rhythm-and-blues	Rhythm-and-blues is a style of popular music that includes elements of blues and African American folk music, characterized by an intense rhythm and a simple chord structure.
Groove	In music, groove is the feeling of a continuous rhythmic pattern created by the focused interaction of the rhythm instruments — piano, guitar, bass, and drums. A listener or dancer responds actively to these repetitive cycles even when musicians shift the tempo or texture in a given song.

Jam session	A jam session is a performance organized by musicians as friendly competition and open to all players. It is characterized by improvisation and meant to test a musician's skill, stamina, and imagination.
Big band	The term "big band" refers to a jazz format of 12-18 musicians organized into sections of instruments (trumpets, saxophones, trombones) and including two or three featured soloists. The "big band era," also called "the swing era," was the predominant form of global popular music between 1930-1945.
Pick-up band	In music, a pick-up band is a group of professional musicians hired for single concert or recording session.
Soul	Soul music is a genre that developed by secularizing the gospel songs of African Americas in the 1950s. It is characterized by intensity of feeling and vocal embellishments and is related to rhythm-and-blues.
Scat	In jazz, "scatting" is a form of vocal improvisation without words. Rather than words, singers use syllables or morphemes to extend the voice as more of an instrument than for the purpose of interpreting lyrics.
Slapstick	Slapstick is a style of humor characterized by exaggerated physical movement or violence that does not lead to any real consequences of pain.
Slap bass	Slap is a technique for playing the acoustic double-bass originally developed in the 1920s by jazz bassists plucking individual strings and letting them resound against the neck, producing a slap.

Ragtime	Ragtime was a popular musical style between 1895 and 1920, often played on piano and featuring syncopated rhythm.
Dropping bombs	"Dropping bombs" refers to a drum technique invented by Kenny Clarke in the 1940s. Instead of supporting the soloist, Clarke challenged musicians with spontaneous, accented hits on the snare or bass drum.
To bend a note	Slide is a musical technique used on guitar to produce evocative, melancholic sounds or new pitches. A "slide" was originally made with the neck of a glass bottle and enabled guitarists to bend notes and play quarter-tones.
Pocket	The term "in the pocket" refers to a relaxed groove created and sustained by the bassist and drummer through rhythms that slightly overlap and yet sound "in sync".
Torch singing	A torch song is one of unrequited or lost love enacted through a vocal style that seemed to reflect the singer's personal experience. The term was invented to describe the vocal styles of Billie Holiday, Sarah Vaughan, Anita O'Day, and Peggy Lee.
EDM	EDM (Electronic Dance Music) is a genre of percussive electronic music intended for discos, rave parties and festivals. They are usually produced by DJs who create multi-track mixes.
Raga	Raga is a melodic framework of improvisation in classical Indian music. In the Indian tradition, melodies are considered to have the ability to "color the mind" and affect the emotions of the audience or individual listeners.

Delta blues	Delta blues is one of the earliest types of country blues, developed by guitarists and harmonica players in the Mississippi River Delta and featuring a rhythmic depth drawn from West African musical practices.
Behind the beat	Playing behind the beat means playing a fraction of a second behind what the rhythm sets, generating anticipation and cross-rhythms.
Walking bass	Walking bass originated in the big band era as a style of bass playing in swing time (4/4) where each note corresponds to one beat, four even beats to each measure.
Shred guitar	An intense style of instrumental playing combining speed, technique, and harmonic complexity. This term is usually associated with heavy metal and rock, but can also be applied to jazz and bluegrass musicians.
Stride piano	Stride piano is a jazz style that developed from ragtime in the 1920s and 1930s, adding more sophisticated rhythm and complex harmonies.
Fill	A fill is a short musical passage, a riff, or a short rhythmic sequence which helps to keep the listener's attention during an interval between melodic phrases.
Juke joint	A juke joint is a small establishment for musical performance with drinking and dancing. It is common in the southern United States, especially in towns with a significant African-American population.

Further reading

Bechet, Sidney. *Treat It Gentle* (Da Capo Pres, 1978).

Becker, Chris. *Freedom of Expression: Interviews With Women in Jazz* (Beckeresque Press, 2015).

Bertholoff, William (Willie "The Lion" Smith), *Music on My Mind* (Da Capo Press, 1978).

Central Avenue Sounds (several authors): *Jazz in Los Angeles* (Oral History), (University of California Press, 1998).

Clarke, Donald. *Billie Holiday: Wishing on the Moon* (Da Capo Pres, 2002).

Dahl, Linda. *Morning Glory: A Biography of Mary Lou Williams* (Pantheon Books, 1999).

Dyer, Geoff, *But Beautiful: A Book About Jazz* (North Point Press, 1991).

Gioia, Ted. *The History of Jazz* (Oxford University Press, 1997).

Goldberg, Joe. *Jazz Masters of the 1950s* (Da Capo Press, 1983).

Hajdu, David. *Lush Life: A Biography of Billy Strayhorn* (Farrar, Straus, Giroux, 1996).

Hentoff, Nat. *Hear Me Talkin' To Ya* (Dover Publications, 1966).

Kahn, Ashley. *A Love Supreme: The Story of John Coltrane's Signature Album* (Penguin Books, 2002).

Lomax, Alan. *Mister Jelly Roll* (University of California Press, 2001).

Murray, Albert. *Stomping the Blues* (Da Capo Press, 1989).

O'Day, Anita. *High Times, Hard Times* (Limelight Edition, 1981).

Ogren, Kathy J. *The Jazz Revolution: Twenties America and the Meaning of Jazz* (Oxford University Press, 1989).

Pepper, Art and Pepper, Laurie. *Straight Life* (G. Schirmer, 1979).

Russell, Ross. *Bird Lives!* (Charterhouse, 1973).

Santoro, Gene. *The Life and Music of Charles Mingus* (Oxford University Press, 2000).

Schuller, Gunther. *Early Jazz* (Oxford University Press, 1968).

Stephen A. *Crist, Dave Brubeck's Time Out* (Oxford University Press, 2019).

Szwed, John. *So What: The Life of Miles Davis* (Billboard Books, 2001).

Taylor, Arthur. *Notes and Tones* (Da Capo Press, 1977).

Teachout, Terry. *Pops: A Life of Louis Armstrong* (Houghton Mifflin Harcourt, 2009).

Quick Immersion Series

For more information, please follow us on Facebook
@TibidaboPublishing or visit www.quickimmersions.com